# CASTLES AND CHURCHES
# OF THE CRUSADING KINGDOM

COLLEGIO NOSTRO
BEATAE MARIAE MAGDALENAE
ANIMO DEVOTO
TAMQUAM MATRI FILII
DEDICAMUS

# CASTLES
# AND CHURCHES
# OF THE CRUSADING
# KINGDOM

BY

T. S. R. BOASE

WITH COLOUR PHOTOGRAPHS BY RICHARD CLEAVE

LONDON
OXFORD UNIVERSITY PRESS
NEW YORK · TORONTO
1967

*Oxford University Press, Ely House, London W. 1*

GLASGOW NEW YORK TORONTO MELBOURNE WELLINGTON
CAPE TOWN SALISBURY IBADAN NAIROBI LUSAKA ADDIS ABABA
BOMBAY CALCUTTA MADRAS KARACHI LAHORE DACCA
KUALA LUMPUR HONG KONG TOKYO

PRINTED IN SWITZERLAND
BY WALTER-VERLAG AG, OLTEN

# CONTENTS

# MAPS

V

# PREFACE

In theory, if frequently not in practice, the principality of Antioch and the counties of Edessa and Tripoli were dependencies of the Latin Kingdom of Jerusalem and are included in the survey given in this book. Later crusading history in Rhodes, Cyprus, and Greece has left many monuments, of considerable interest if generally, with the exception of Rhodes and Budrum, of no great merit; but these, later in time and subject to very different influences, are not dealt with here.

I have attempted some consistency in the transliteration of Arab names, based on *The History of the Crusades* published by the University of Pennsylvania Press (Vol. I 1955, Vol. II 1962), but I doubt if I have achieved it. Where the crusading name for a town or castle has some established familiarity, I have used it. In the quotations I have retained the forms used by the authors, which will serve to show the great diversity of practice in this matter.

The colour photographs were taken by Surgeon Lieutenant-Commander Cleave, R.N., on a journey which is in the direct succession to those described in chapter II.

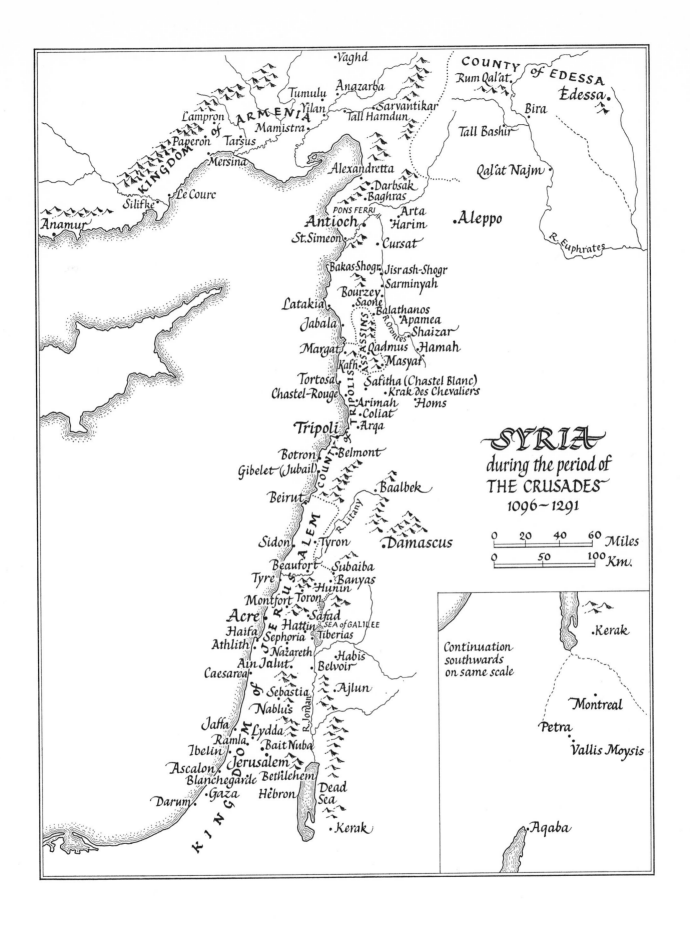

Vaghd

COUNTY OF EDESSA

Tumulu · Anazarba
Yilan · Rum Qal'at · Edessa ·
· Sarvantikar · Bira
Lampron · ARMENIA · Tall Hamdun · Tall Bashir
Mamistra
Paperon · Tarsus · KINGDOM OF · Qal'at Najm ·
Mersina · Alexandretta
· Darbsak · Aleppo
Le Courc · Baghras
Silifke · PONS FERRI · Arta
Anamur · Antioch · Harim R. Euphrates
St. Simeon · Cursat

Bakas-Shogr · Jisr ash-Shogr
· Sarminyah
Bourzey · Balathanos
Latakia · Saone · Apamea
Jabala · R. Orontes · Shaizar
Margat · ASSASSINS · Qadmus · Hamah
Kafh · Masyaf
Tortosa · Safitha (Chastel Blanc)
Chastel-Rouge · Krak des Chevaliers
· Arimah · Homs
· Coliat
COUNTY OF TRIPOLIS · Arqa
Tripoli
Botron · Belmont
Gibelet (Jubail) · Baalbek

Beirut R. Litany
Sidon · Tyron · Damascus
Beaufort · Subaiba
Tyre · Banyas
Montfort · Toron · Hunin
Acre · Safad
Hattin · SEA of GALILEE
Haifa · Sephoria · Tiberias
Athlith · Nazareth
Ain Jalut · Habis
Caesarea · Belvoir
· Sebastia · Ajlun
· Nablus
Jaffa · Lydda
Ramla · Bait Nuba
Ibelin · KINGDOM OF JERUSALEM
Ascalon · Jerusalem
Blanchegarde · Bethlehem
Darum · Gaza · Hebron Dead
Sea
· Kerak

SYRIA
during the period of
THE CRUSADES
1096–1291

0   20   40   60 Miles
0      50     100 Km.

Continuation
southwards
on same scale

· Kerak

· Montreal

Petra ·
· Vallis Moysis

· Aqaba

1095
Urban II preaches the crusade at the Council of Clermont.

1097
First crusade reaches Constantinople: Alexius Comnenus Emperor, 1081–1118.

1097, 21 October–1098, 3 June
Siege of Antioch.

1099, 15 July
Capture of Jerusalem: Godfrey of Bouillon elected Advocate of the Sepulchre.

1100
Death of Godfrey: Baldwin I (1100–1118) succeeds as king.

1109
Capture of Tripoli.

1115
Baldwin I builds castle of Montreal.

1118
Accession of Baldwin II (1118–1131).

1124
Capture of Tyre.

1131
Accession of Fulk of Anjou (1131–1143), as husband of Melisend, daughter of Baldwin II.

1132/3
The Assassins settle in the Anṣārīyah mountains.

1142
Castle of Kerak built: Krak des Chevaliers ceded to the Hospitallers.

1143
Death of Fulk, accession of Baldwin III (1143 to 1163).

1144
Zengi captures Edessa.

1147/8
Second crusade, led by the Emperor Conrad III and Louis VII of France.

1149, 15 July
Dedication of Church of Holy Sepulchre.

1153
Capture of Ascalon.

1154
Damascus submits to Nūr-ad-Dīn.

1155
Crusading alliance with Manuel Comnenus (1143 to 1180).

1163
Accession of Amalric (1163–1174).

1163–69
Campaigns against Egypt.

1169
Saladin occupies Cairo for Nūr-ad-Dīn.

1174
Death of Nūr-ad-Dīn; and of Amalric: accession of Baldwin IV, the Leper (1174–1185).

1186
Margat ceded to the Hospitallers.

1187, 4 July
Defeat of crusading army by Saladin at Hattin.

1187, 2 October
Jerusalem surrenders to Saladin.

1188
Saladin's northern campaign: capture of Saone; and of Kerak.

1189
Guy of Lusignan begins siege of Acre.

1190
Death of Frederick Barbarossa in Cilicia.

1191
Arrivals of Philip II of France and Richard Cœur-de-Lion at Acre: recapture of Acre by the crusaders: departure of Philip.

1192
Guy of Lusignan buys Cyprus from the Templars, to whom Richard had assigned it after his conquest of the island: departure of Richard: refortification of Kerak by al-ʿĀdil.

1193
Death of Saladin.

1198
Leo II crowned king of Armenia (1198–1219).

1200
al-ʿĀdil, Saladin's brother, proclaimed Sultan of Egypt and Syria.

1204
Constantinople taken by the crusaders.

1217–18
Crusade of Andrew of Hungary.

1218
Death of al-ʿĀdil: al-Kāmil succeeds him in Egypt.

1219
Capture of Damietta by crusaders.

1221
Crusaders evacuate Damietta.

1229
Frederick II regains Jerusalem, Nazareth, and Toron by treaty with al-Kāmil.

1232–36
John of Ibelin leads the baronage against Frederick's bailie, Richard Filangieri.

1239–40
Crusade of Theobald of Champagne: treaties with Damascus and Egypt restore Galilee and Ascalon to the crusaders: Jerusalem occupied by an-Nāṣir of Kerak.

1244
Jerusalem sacked by Khorezmians: Egyptians and Khorezmians defeat a crusader-Syrian army at Gaza.

1249
Louis IX lands in Egypt and captures Damietta.

1250
Louis defeated and captured by Egyptians; ransomed by surrender of Damietta.

1250–54
Louis in Palestine.

1258
Hulagu and the Mongols capture Baghdad and kill last ʿAbbāsid caliph.

1259
Kutuz becomes first Mamluk sultan.

1260
Mongols under Kitbogha take Damascus, but are defeated at ʿAin Jālūt by Mamluk army under Baybars: Baybars kills Kutuz and succeeds him as sultan (1260–1277).

1261
Michael Palaeologus reconquers Constantinople.

1266
Mamluks under Kalavun devastate Armenia: Baybars captures Safad and overruns Galilee.

1268
Baybars captures Jaffa, Beaufort, and Antioch.

1270–72
Crusade of Edward of England.

1271
Baybars takes Krak des Chevaliers.

1277
Death of Baybars: succeeded after two years of dispute by Kalavun.

1281
Kalavun defeats the Mongols near Homs.

1285
Kalavun takes Margat.

1287
Fall of Latakia.

1289
Kalavun captures Tripoli.

1290
Death of Kalavun: succeeded by his son, al-Ashraf Khalil.

1291, 18 May
Khalil captures Acre: Athlith and Tortosa evacuated.

1307–14
Suppression of the order of the Temple.

1309
Hospitallers occupy Rhodes.

Jerusalem with the Church of the Holy Sepulchre

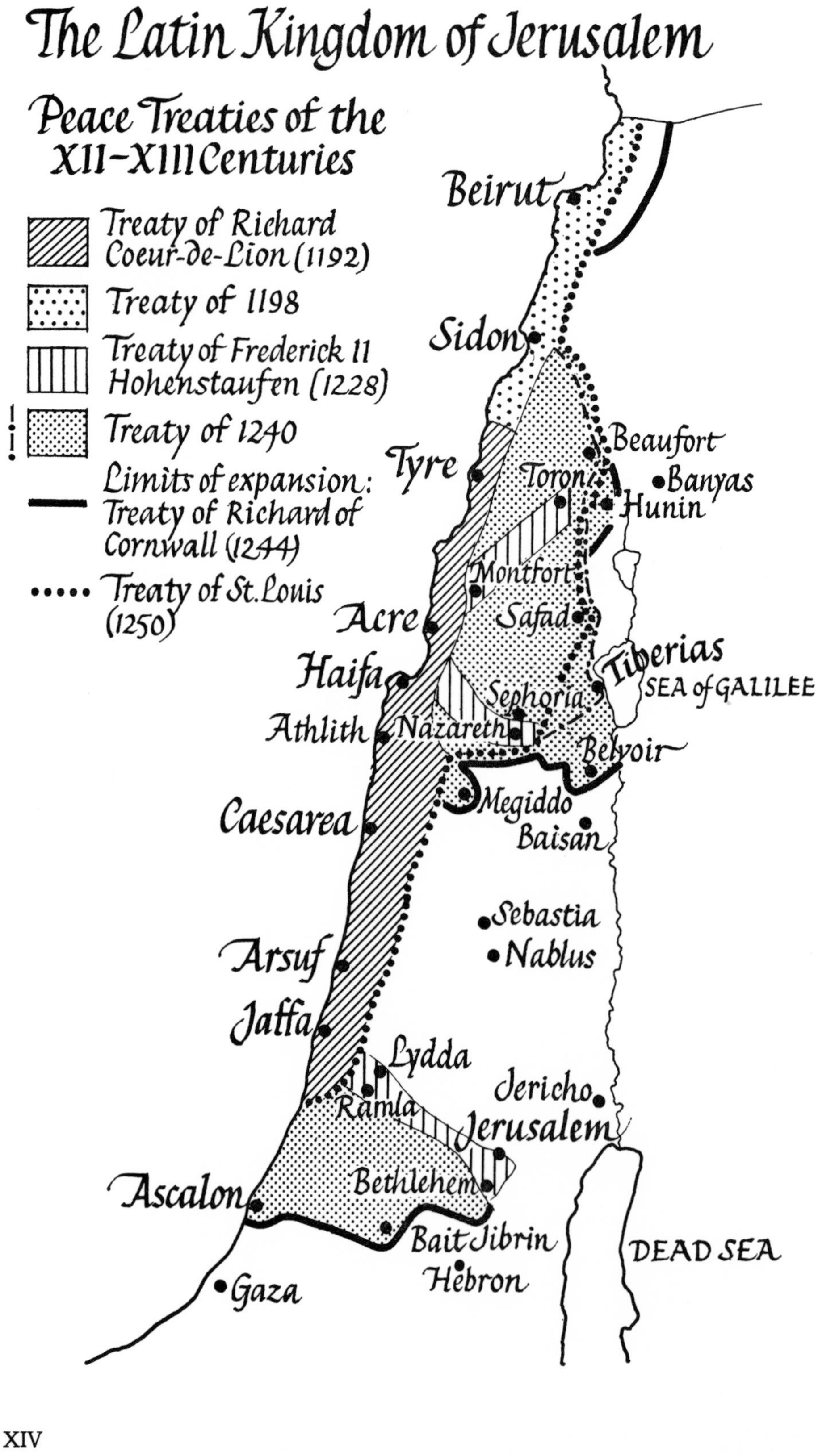

# The Latin Kingdom of Jerusalem

## Peace Treaties of the XII–XIII Centuries

Treaty of Richard Coeur-de-Lion (1192)

Treaty of 1198

Treaty of Frederick II Hohenstaufen (1228)

Treaty of 1240

Limits of expansion: Treaty of Richard of Cornwall (1244)

Treaty of St. Louis (1250)

Beirut

Sidon

Tyre

Beaufort

Toron

Banyas

Hunin

Montfort

Safad

Acre

Haifa

Sephoria

Tiberias

SEA of GALILEE

Athlith

Nazareth

Belvoir

Caesarea

Megiddo

Baisan

Sebastia

Nablus

Arsuf

Jaffa

Lydda

Jericho

Ramla

Jerusalem

Ascalon

Bethlehem

Bait Jibrin

Hebron

DEAD SEA

Gaza

# CONTENTS

## MAPS

# JERUSALEM

*St. Jerome tells us that we read in ancient histories about men who have visited countries and crossed seas to the end that they might behold with their eyes the things whereof they had read in books. ... What wonder, then, if Christians long to behold and visit the land whereof all Christ's Churches tell us? The men of old venerated the Holy of Holies, because therein was the ark of the covenant, the cherubim with the mercy-seat, the manna, and Aaron's rod that flowered—all of which were types of things to come. Is not Christ's sepulchre more to be worshipped by us, which, whenever any man enters, so many times seeth he with his mind's eyes the Saviour lying there wrapped in linen clothes? And when he has gone a little further, he sees the stone rolled away, and the angel sitting thereon, and showing to the women the napkin with the grave-clothes. What Christian, when he has seen these, would not hasten to come unto Bethlehem, to see the Babe weeping in the manger; Mary brought to bed in the inn beneath the hollow rock, which is to be seen at this day; the angels singing glory to God and peace to men in the presence of the shepherds; and, greatest wonder of all, to see the three Magi in their noble majesty kneeling before the manger, with no roof above their heads save the overhanging rock? Thence let him return to Jerusalem, that he may see and hear Jesus preaching in the Temple, teaching His disciples on the Mount of Olives, supping on Mount Sion, washing His disciples' feet, giving them His Body and Blood, praying in Gethsemane, sweating blood, kissing His betrayer, being dragged away prisoner, mocked, spat upon, judged, bearing His cross, sinking beneath the weight of the cross before the very gate of the city that is to be seen at this day, helped by Simon of Cyrene, and for our sake celebrating the mysteries of His Passion on Calvary. The memory of each and every one of these places is still as full and complete as it was on that day when these things were done therein. ... Seeing, however, that some are possessed by a desire to picture to their minds those things which they are not able to behold with their eyes, and wishing to fulfil their longing, as far as in me lieth, I have, to the best of my ability, thought about, diligently taken note of, and laboriously described that land, over which my feet have often passed; for I would have the reader to know that I have set down in this my description nought save what I have either seen with mine own eyes, when at the place itself, or, when I could not come at it, what I have seen from some neighbouring mountain-top or other convenient place, and have carefully noted the answers given by the Syrian or Saracen, or other people of the land, whom I most diligently questioned. Indeed, as I have already said, I have either walked on foot all over the whole land, from Dan to Beersheba, from the Dead Sea to the Mediterranean Sea, which are its boundaries, or else I have carefully made inquiries about the places which I could not come at.*[1]

Thus wrote Burchard of Mount Sion, who had come from Magdeburg or the regions round and settled for some years in Jerusalem, after 1271 and before 1291, that is in the closing period of the crusading occupation, when Jerusalem was in Moslem hands and Acre, the last town held by the Christians, hard pressed and near its final capture on 18 May 1291. This longing *to behold and visit the land* had been a potent force from much earlier times, even before the Bordeaux pilgrim in 333 had written his *Itinerarium a Burdigala Hierusalem usque*, the first guide book to the Holy Land. St. Jerome in 386 could write of the many *bishops, martyrs, the men eloquent in ecclesiastical learning who had come to Jerusalem* to complete their knowledge of Christ. Despite the Arab conquest, with the consequent increased dangers of the journey, travellers still came on their quest. About the year 668, thirty years after Omar had captured the city, Arculf, a French bishop, visited Jerusalem and on his return journey his ship was driven out of its course and wrecked on the island of Iona. There to the local abbot, Adamnan, Arculf related his pilgrimage and drew a plan of the Church of the Holy Sepulchre which

Adamnan embodied in his book *De locis sanctis,* and the Venerable Bede in Northumbria read of it and repeated much of the account in his own writings.[2]

With the crusading occupation of Palestine in 1099, pilgrimage gained both new obligations and facilities. Accounts of the Holy Land from the twelfth and thirteenth centuries are numerous and detailed. They were still however written for spiritual edification, as testimony to Gospel truth, and little is said of the actual buildings seen. The visible and tangible to an illiterate age were strong proofs of Holy Writ, not to be lightly set aside on grounds of probability. Archaeological interests, in our acceptance of the term, were almost non-existent. The builders of the crusading kingdom destroyed the historical evidence of ancient monuments with unhesitating readiness, and any claim of a site to particular sanctity at once led to its transformation into Romanesque or Gothic terms. By the time that some attempts were made at accurate description, the local colour had been immensely altered. *Those natural forms,* wrote George Sandys who was in Jerusalem in 1611, *are utterly deformed, which would have better satisfied the beholder; and too much regard hath made them less regardable.*[3]

THE HOLY SEPULCHRE      To pilgrims and crusaders the Church of the Holy Sepulchre was the final object of their devotions; it was the Via Sancti Sepulchri that they felt called upon to take. They were untroubled by any doubts, historical or archaeological, as to the survival of the rock-cut tomb and the persistence of knowledge of its location. We, trained to scholarly doubt, cannot but wonder whether this was in fact the right place. Historically, leaving aside all doctrinal implications, it is reasonably well attested that Jesus of Nazareth, the leader of a religious movement and the propounder of teachings that have profoundly searched the minds of men, was crucified probably in A.D. 29, certainly between A.D. 26 and 36, at a place called Golgotha, and was buried in a tomb in a nearby garden. Places of execution and burial would both have been outside the walls of the town, and much research has gone to establishing the fact that the present Golgotha originally was outside the city. This is supported by considerable archaeological evidence. The site of Jerusalem has varied considerably amongst its hills. Certainly the circuit of the walls was increased by Herod Agrippa I c. A.D. 40, and the present enclosed area represents the rebuilding of Jerusalem as Aelia Capitolina by Hadrian in 135. The authenticity of the present site is possible on those grounds, but depends finally on a tradition, in the transmission of which there are some, though not considerable, gaps. When Titus took and destroyed Jerusalem in 70, the early Christian community appears already to have fled to Pella and there is no clear evidence of their return before 122. In the third century there are mentions, particularly in the writings of Origen (d. 254), of a growing cult of pilgrimage to the scenes of Christ's ministry, but the emphasis on an accepted tradition is related to the cave at Bethlehem, not to the tomb at Golgotha. For this there may well have been good reason. In the rebuilding of Jerusalem under Hadrian the site or neighbourhood of the site, where the church of the Sepulchre was later to stand, had been levelled as a forum with at its eastern end shrines of Jupiter, Juno, and Venus, and therefore was peculiarly repugnant and, at least to those of native Jewish birth, inaccessible to Christians. It is, however, more probable that the place of the tomb should have been known to them, than that it should have gone from memory. Certainly when Constantine undertook the re-sanctification of the spot, there was little doubt where to look. *The pious Emperor,* wrote Eusebius of Caesarea, a Palestinian contemporary of the event, *judged it incumbent on him to render the blessed locality of our Saviour's Resurrection an object of attraction and veneration to all. He issued injunctions therefore for the building of a house of prayer.*[4] The tomb, Eusebius tells us, had been completely buried *by the ungodly men who set themselves to assign to darkness and oblivion that divine monument of immortality.* A cave sepulchre was certainly discovered in the Constantinian excavations, and the rock round it was cut away leaving it as a detached feature, encased in a small edicule, and

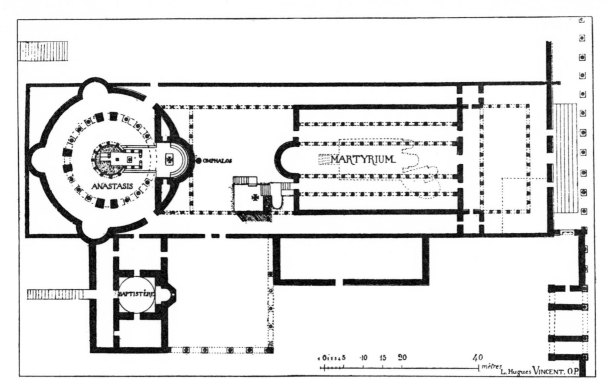

Plan of the Church of the Holy Sepulchre, 634 to 1009, after PP. Vincent and Abel

framed to the west by a hemicycle of walls, with a central apse and an apse at each end of the half circle; to the east was a large basilica, known as the Martyrium, with a single apse at its western end, opening into an atrium, approached through an impressive triple entrance, parts of which still survive in the Russian hospice. To secure the level platform necessary for this complex of buildings, the gully and rock quarries between the slope containing the tomb and hill of Calvary were partially filled by earth and rubble, partially by arched supporting structures, though some of this levelling may have been done under Hadrian. The rocky hillock, or possibly a spur projecting from the main slope, known as Calvary, rose, at least on three sides, to a height of about thirty feet, and in the Constantinian plan the summit was left uncovered in the open space between the hemicycle and the Martyrium.

The tomb is the principal feature in Eusebius's account, but veneration of Calvary soon ran it close. Etheria in the account of her pilgrimage (383–85) refers to services commemorating the finding of the True Cross, and the cult of this relic, ignored by Eusebius, added new importance to the site of the Crucifixion. Rufinus (d. c. 410), the continuator of Eusebius's *History,* has the full story of the miraculous finding of the cross by St. Helena, a story that was to have such lasting fascination for Western artists, whereas Eusebius has contented himself with an account of the venerable lady visiting Palestine and founding churches on the sites of the Nativity, Ascension, and Eleona, the scene of Christ's preaching on the Mount of Olives. Legends and identifications were, however, growing with abandon. The *Breviarius de Hierosolyma* of 530 cites among other interesting relics the charger on which the head of St. John was carried, the horn with which David and Solomon were anointed, and (from the Gospel of James or some other apocryphal source) the dried blood of Zacharias, slain before the altar.

Constantine's church was to stand for barely three hundred years. On 4 May 614 the Persian army under Chosroes II captured Jerusalem, partially destroyed the basilica and carried off its treasure,

3

including the True Cross, later won back by Heraclius, who in 629 carried it barefoot into Jerusalem. The patriarch Modestus (d. 634) restored the buildings, on the whole making little change in the Constantinian plan, though almost certainly the rotunda was enlarged and completely covered. Then in 637 Jerusalem passed under Arab control. On the whole Christian pilgrimage was tolerated, and the buildings round the Sepulchre left undisturbed, though during riots in 966 the doors and roofs were burnt and the Patriarch executed on the parvis or courtyard before the church. In 1009, however, the Fatimide caliph, al-Ḥākim, whose disordered mind was unpredictable in its workings, issued orders for the complete destruction of the Christian churches in Jerusalem. This was a thorough and effective demolition, very different from the sack by the Persians, and the ruins were not readily repaired. Radulph Glaber, who heard it from Odoric, bishop of Orleans, gives a touching account of the crowds of pilgrims in 1033, held to be the thousandth anniversary of the Crucifixion, and of the indignities they suffered.[5] In the following year a severe earthquake completed the devastation. It was not till 1048, when quieter times prevailed, that the patriarch Nicephorus, largely financed by the Emperor Constantine Monomachus, undertook a new restoration. The ruins of the domed rotunda were reconstructed, supported on a circle of eighteen pillars, with the edicule of the tomb as its central feature. The main altar was in a polygonal apse, projecting on the western face from a straight wall with four doorways, stretches of wall that still survive with their upper windows visible above later rebuilding. There was no attempt to rebuild the Martyrium.

Such was the state of the church as the crusaders found it, on that 15 July 1099, when, cleansing themselves and their garments from the traces of a horrible massacre, they came *rejoicing and weeping from excess of gladness to worship at the Sepulchre of our Saviour Jesus*. The tomb chamber seems to have been their earliest care. Fearing Latin cupidity, the Greek and Syrian patriarchs had removed and hidden the actual, or traditionally the actual, slab on which Christ's body had lain, but this was soon found, and a new edicule replaced the circular, pillared cupola. The crusading shrine was rectangular, ending in a pentagonal apse, with a small cupola raised on colonettes and surmounted by a silver figure of Christ, larger than life, which was replaced some time before 1172 by a golden cross. When Abbot Daniel of Kiev visited Jerusalem in 1106 the tomb, both inside and out, was encased in marble, though the rock could be seen through some small apertures. This was a necessary precaution to prevent pilgrims chipping it away. Brother James of Verona in 1335 describes how he provided himself with iron chisels, and, while his companions distracted the guardians, secured several pieces of the rock of Calvary. He complains of the hardness of the stone of the column of flagellation, which foiled his attempts: *satis laboravi et nichil profuit*.[6] Despite all precautions stones from the Sepulchre long remained popular relics. William Wey, a fellow of Eton who travelled to Palestine in 1458 and again in 1462, left in his will a stone from the Sepulchre and one from Calvary.[7] Their genuineness can hardly be accepted without hesitation, particularly by anyone familiar with the continuous huckstering on historic sites of the Near East.

We have nothing that can be taken as a realistic drawing of the Sepulchre till those of Giovanni Zuallardo and Bernardo Amico in 1585 and 1609 respectively, both after its exterior had been much restored in 1555, though along the lines of the earlier building. Zuallardo and Amico disagree as to whether or not the arcade and cupola arches were round or pointed: Amico, who shows it with pointed arches, is the more careful draftsman, and is borne out by a drawing made by Ladislaus Mayer in 1748.[8] Lancet arches on the edicule, even if one assumes its restoration to date from the opening years of the twelfth century, are not in themselves improbable. The pointed arch was known in the Near East since at least the end of the ninth century, and the cistern at Ramla, known as St. Helena's, built in stone with slightly intersecting arches, may be even earlier. Syrian stonemasons must

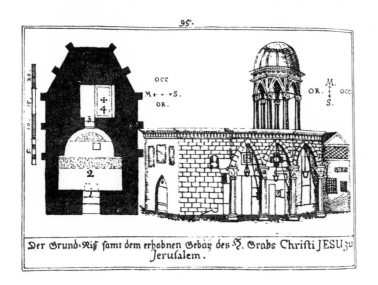

Edicule of the Tomb. Ladislaus Mayer (1748)

have been familiar with this method, and with few exceptions the Franks employed the pointed arch in their churches and used it frequently in their rebuilding of the church of the Holy Sepulchre. In 1808 the edicule and the greater part of the rotunda were destroyed by fire, and the present tomb edicule is a singularly unfortunate erection in nineteenth-century Levantine taste.

In 1114 the patriarch Arnulf, having at last overcome the main opposition to his claims, reorganized the chapter of the cathedral and imposed on it the Augustinian rule of communal life. Foucher of Chartres tells us of a severe earthquake which shook Jerusalem in 1106, and the still ruinous buildings of the Holy Sepulchre must have suffered from it. More settled circumstances provided an opportunity for the urgent needs of restoration. If the crusading chapter were aware of the Constantinian layout, they were certainly not in any way influenced by it. The site of the Martyrium was not re-used and instead the crusading choir was placed in the former colonnaded court between the rotunda and the Martyrium. This made it possible to combine it with the rotunda in one building. The eastern apse of

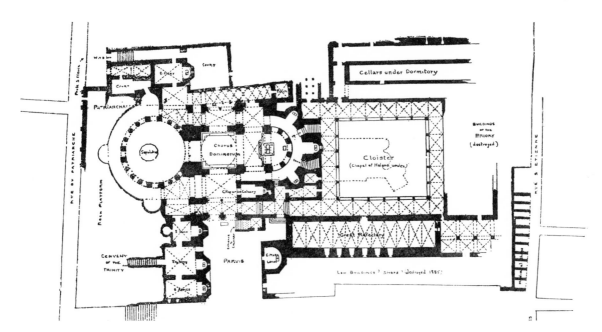

Plan of Crusading Church of the Holy Sepulchre

Interior section of the Church of the Holy Sepulchre. Bernardo Amico (1609)

the former was removed and replaced by an archway leading into a crossing, covered by a dome, beyond which was the choir and semicircular presbytery, the latter with an ambulatory from which opened three radiating chapels: to the south-east a flight of steps led to the chapel of Calvary, and the south transept ended in a double doorway which formed the main entrance: to the north the design of the transept was complicated by the retention of the old Byzantine colonnade, forming a second row of pillars slightly off the main crusading axis, which was governed by the eastern orientation of the new choir, whereas in the Constantinian Martyrium the altar had been in the west wall, that is orientated towards the actual Sepulchre. Over the crossing connecting the two buildings was raised a tall dome, carried on a drum with pointed arcading, pierced with eight pointed windows and supported on pendentives. The transepts, choir, and apse have ogival vaults with finely moulded ribs. The stones are laid horizontally in the French fashion and their rough finish suggests that the vaults were originally plastered. From various accounts of the splendour of the interior decoration, they were almost certainly painted. These vaults are similar in design to those that Suger was introducing at St. Denis almost contemporaneously with the building in Jerusalem, for St. Denis was consecrated in 1144, the Church of the Holy Sepulchre on 15 July 1149, the fiftieth anniversary of the taking of the city. Externally the roofs are flat in accordance with Palestinian practice, so that no sloping roof limited the tribune gallery space, and the tribune openings are almost equal in scale to the aisle bays beneath them. Throughout the arched openings are slightly pointed. Originally the church must have been well lit, but the blocking of the choir arcade and of many of the windows has created the present obscure gloom, which pervades the building and serves at least to hide some of the miserable changes that disfigure it since the rebuilding after the fire of 1808.

Opposite page: The façade of the south transept of the Church of the Holy Sepulchre

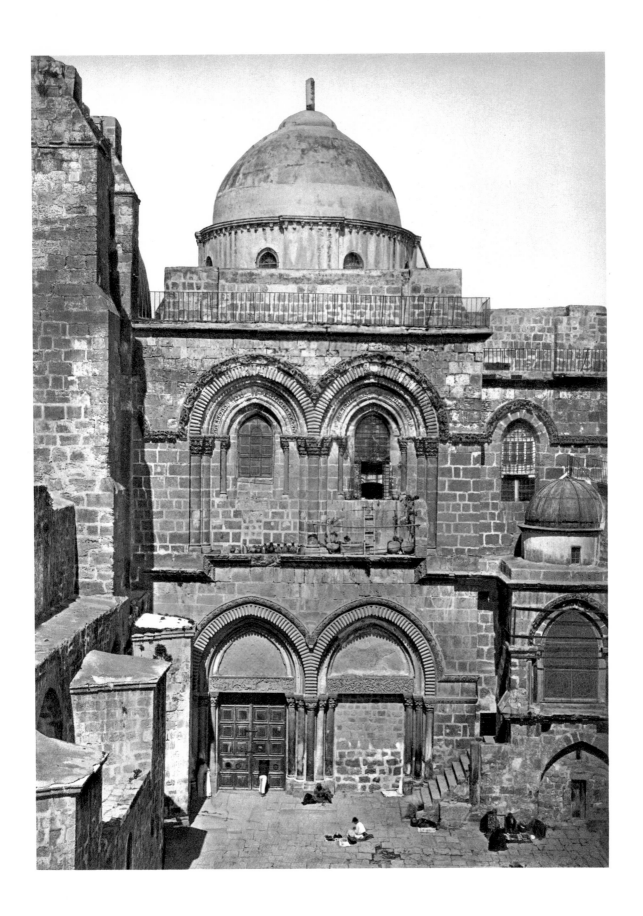

In the interior some of the carved capitals are certainly re-used Byzantine work, particularly the magnificent examples in the underground chapel of St. Helena, the site of the finding of the Cross: others are medieval, including one in the north transept, where a crowned and winged figure, possibly Solomon, is stylistically in keeping with French contemporary work. In the cloister, beyond the eastern apse, some curious capitals survive, awkwardly fitted on bent-armed consols, which must be local work by masons unused to the tradition required from them.

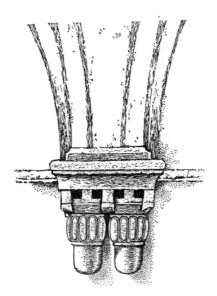

Capital in the cloister of the Church of the Holy Sepulchre

Mosaic and painting also played a great part in the decorative scheme. One must imagine the Church of the Holy Sepulchre glowing with all the subdued richness with which we are familiar in St. Mark's at Venice. Abbot Daniel describing the rotunda in 1106 lists figures of apostles in the arches above the tribune, and a considerable iconographic scheme, centring on the Anastasis, Christ releasing the souls of the just from limbo, above the altar. This was on the wall removed to make the opening through to the crusaders' church, but similar designs seem to have been used, possibly re-used, by the crusaders in their apse: references to the mosaics continue to be made until the seventeenth century, by which time they were much obliterated. The crusaders, or at least some of them, seem to have been fascinated by this Byzantine inheritance, for William of Tyre tells us how Godfrey of Bouillon's companions used to complain of the time he spent in churches, asking about the meaning of each image and picture. Paintings *(iconae)*, presumably on panels, were also employed hanging from the arches. Of all this lavish decoration, there exists today only a fragment in mosaic in the chapel of Calvary, showing Christ in Glory. Finely drawn, it could be either Byzantine work of the mid-eleventh century, or crusader-Byzantine work of the mid-twelfth, probably the latter, for the inscription is in Latin.

The main façade opened on the parvis or court of access on the south side. George Sandys describes it as follows: *The Frontispiece opposing the South, of an excellent Structure; having two joyning doors, the one now walled up, supported with Columns of Marble, over which a Transom engraven with historical Figures; the Walls and Arches crested and garnished with Flority. On the left hand there standeth a Tower, now something ruined (once, as some say, a Steeple, and deprived by Saladine of Bells, unsufferable to the Mahometans:) on the right hand, by certain steps, a little Chappel is ascended; coupled above, and sustained at the corners with Pillars of Marble. Below, thorow a Wall, which bounds the East-side of the Court, a pair of stairs do mount to the top of the Rock (yet no Rock evident:) where is a little Chappel built (as they say) in the place where Abraham*

Opposite page: Doorways of the Church of the Holy Sepulchre

9

*would have sacrificed Isaac; of much devotion, and kept by the Priest of the Abissines. This joyneth to the top of the Temple, level, and (if I forget not) floored with Plaister. Out of the Temple there arise two ample Cupuloes: that next the East (covering the East-end and Iles of the Chappel) to be ascended by steps on the outside: the other over the Church of the Sepulchre, being open in the middle.*[9] This description still fits the existing edifice. Sandys' phrase *garnished with Flority* is a picturesque term for the elaborate friezes, much influenced by classical prototypes such as can still be seen at Baalbek, Tyre, and elsewhere, that divide the façade into its two stages and provide a cornice below the dome. Deeply undercut, large in scale, inventive in design, the friezes of the south façade are outstanding examples of a Franco-Byzantine style, and appear to be the product of a mason's yard where local carvers were employed under Western supervision. The most developed example of it is appropriately the tympanum to the chapel of Calvary, where vine tendrils curve in rhythmic profusion, the True Vine thus placed on the entrance to the scene of the Atonement. Below the string courses of the doors and windows are voussoirs formed of godrons, or rows of deeply bevelled stones, a style popular in the Near East, found in much medieval work in Cairo, and used contemporaneously with crusading buildings by the Normans in Sicily, along with other motifs of Arab inspiration. The capitals of the doorways have windswept acanthus leaves, similar to those at St. Mark's in Venice, and certainly based on Byzantine examples. Taken as a whole, this façade is a Romanesque design such as might be expected in Southern France, but the arches throughout are slightly pointed. The crusaders themselves broke the symmetry of the design by building their bell tower, which cuts into the friezes, blocking a window still visible

Carving on doorway of the Church of the Holy Sepulchre

from within. The *Transom engraven with historical Figures* has now been moved to the Rockefeller Museum in Jerusalem, but before this it had probably undergone some alteration. Fra Niccolò da Poggibonsi in 1345 described the scenes shown as the Raising of Lazarus, the Palm Sunday Entry, the Last Supper, and the Betrayal. The first three subjects can still be seen on the lintel from the western door, but that from the eastern is a completely different design of figures and beasts in interlacing scrolls, a notable piece of twelfth-century carving, but hardly suited to its position and in fact not exactly worked to fit it. It seems likely that the original slab, beginning with the Betrayal, showed scenes of the Passion, and that, owing to decay or Moslem vandalism, it was at some time replaced by the existing carving, more pagan in feeling and less obnoxious to Moslem susceptibilities. Underneath, the central pillar of the doorway is poised on a crag of rock jutting out into the vaulted chamber built between Calvary and the hillside of the tomb. The

Carving from the façade of the Church of the Holy Sepulchre

lower side of the rock has been smoothed off so that a supporting block could be placed beneath, but this support was never provided, perhaps through lack of building supervision, till it was at last built in 1962, when the substructures were cleared and investigated. Now from these foundations it is possible to look up and see the rocky hill of Calvary rising from near its original ground level into the encasing chapel above. To anyone who has had the opportunity of exploring this long inaccessible basement it is difficult not to accept that this is the veritable place of the Crucifixion.

Endless visitors have paused and meditated as from the parvis they looked up at the storeys of the façade, outlined by their carved dripstones, with, below, the entrance doorways, so long guarded by Moslem warders. Some like Ludolph of Suchem in 1350 sought to link it with more familiar settings: *Above the Mount Calvary and Christ's sepulchre a great and fair church has been built, nobly decorated with marble, mosaic work, paintings and other ornaments. It has towers in front of the choir and above the same, and it is open above the place of Christ's sepulchre. The inside of this church is very much like the cathedral of Munster in Westphalia, especially in the choir.*[10]

Alphonse de Lamartine, nearly five hundred years later, gives a more complex emotional reaction clothed in elaborate, poetic prose, whose rhythms are not easily turned into an English form:

*The church of the Holy Sepulchre has been often and so well described, that I shall not describe it anew. It is, on the exterior especially, a vast and fine monument of the Byzantine epoch; the architecture is grave, solemn, grandiose and rich for the time of its building; it is a worthy pavilion cast by the piety of men over the tomb of the Son of Man. In comparing this church with what the same age has produced, one finds it superior to all. Santa Sophia may be more colossal, but it is more barbarous in its shape; it is, without, only a mountain of stones flanked by hills of stone; the Holy Sepulchre, on the contrary, is a cupola, ethereal and chiselled, where the skilful grace of the carving on doors, windows, capitals and cornices is become lace-work to be worthy of taking its place in this monument to the supreme thought of humanity; where inspiration is written in the parts as in the whole of the building. It is true that the church of the Holy Sepulchre is not such today as it was when St. Helena, mother of Constantine, constructed it; the kings of Jerusalem retouched it and embellished it with ornaments of this half Western, half Moorish architecture, for which they had found the liking and the models in the East. But such as now it is, on the exterior, its Byzantine mass, its Greek, Gothic and arabesque decorations, with its scars even, stigmata of time and barbarity, which remain imprinted on its façade, it is in no contradiction with the thought that one brings to it, with the thought that it expresses; there is before it no painful feeling of a great idea ill interpreted, of a great memory profaned by the hands of men: on the contrary, instinctively one says: 'This is what I looked for.' Man has made of his best. The monument is not worthy of the tomb, but it is worthy of this human race which has wished to honour the great sepulchre, and, under the impact of this first and solemn impression, one passes into the sombre, vaulted vestibule of the nave.*[11]

The Church of the Holy Sepulchre. Woodcut by Erhard Rewich, c. 1485

The Church
of St. Anne, Jerusalem

Of the many other medieval churches of Jerusalem, some are completely destroyed and their sites
matter of dispute, others almost completely rebuilt. The Armenian church of St. James is a twelfth-
century building, and some of the details, such as the godrons of the south doorway, are clearly
influenced by crusading examples, but the plan, an inscribed cross, and the central cupola belong to the
Armenian not the Western tradition. Some of the capitals, one of which has curious, dog-like creatures
carved on it, are undoubtedly twelfth-century work.

The church of St. Anne, the best preserved of the Jerusalem churches, must have been built by the
masons of the Holy Sepulchre, for, on a much simplified scale, its west façade echoes the design of the
greater church and its upper window has godroned voussoirs and a head-mould of stiff leaf acanthus.
It was the church of a nunnery that enjoyed royal favour and owned a market in Jerusalem, where
several arches in the Sūq al-ʿAttarīn are still carved with its name, 'Sca Anna'. Disappropriated by
Saladin, whose inscription establishing it as a *madrasah* still fills the central tympanum, it remained
comparatively undamaged until in 1835, during the occupation of Jerusalem by Ibrahim Pasha, the
convent buildings were pulled down to provide stones for a barracks. The church was used as a stable,
and refuse was dumped round it to such a height that it was possible to climb over the mounds on to
the terraces of the roof. Then in 1856 it was, at the instigation of some French archaeologists, ceded
to France as a token of Turkish appreciation of the part played by France in the Crimean war. It was
placed in the charge of the order of White Fathers, and a thorough restoration was undertaken between
1862 and 1877. Today it is the most complete example of a twelfth-century crusading church.

13

Opposite the south front of the church of the Holy Sepulchre stood a complex of buildings centring round the Hospital, the charitable undertaking that had almost certainly been organized by merchants of Amalfi before the crusades, but which with the appointment about 1120 of Raymond du Puy as grand master had developed into a military and political force of great significance in the kingdom. Here were the churches of St. Mary the Great, St. Mary Latin, and St. John the Baptist. Of these the church of St. John is completely rebuilt, and St. Mary the Great, though its bell tower was still standing in the mid-nineteenth century, has left not even any certainty as to its exact site or plan. Of St. Mary Latin some carvings, voussoirs with signs of the Zodiac, and fragments of a tympanum, are fitted into the doorway of the German Lutheran church of the Redeemer, built in 1898; and in the small restored cloister there are medieval capitals. From these buildings must come also the magnificent acanthus capitals preserved in the convent of St. Abraham, on the east side of the parvis, and in the Museum of the Greek Patriarchate. It is always a problem to decide whether such capitals are re-used Byzantine work or crusading versions of a style that so deeply impressed them. The latter tend to have deeper indentations between the volutes, but, cut from the same building stone by masons working in a strong local tradition, it is hard to draw clear distinctions. Nor is the tool work a certain guide: the older capitals required adjustment to new positions, and the particular hatching of the crusaders, recognizable by the spacing of the teeth of the small rake that they used, often appears on them. The Greek Patriarchate has also some pieces of figure sculpture, of unrecorded provenance but probably from the Hospital site, some of it of high quality, particularly a slab in high relief with an archer and his dog, as vivid and muscularly taut as anything in medieval sculpture, and a voussoir of a headless figure, where the robes are carved in typical Romanesque patterns. Two sadly mutilated capitals have scenes from the life of the Baptist, and must come from the church dedicated to him. In the Louvre is a fragment of Christ on the ass, found by Clermont-Ganneau in 1873, which he hoped was a missing piece of the lintel of the church of the Holy Sepulchre, but the scale makes this impossible and it must come from some other rendering of the Palm Sunday Entry.

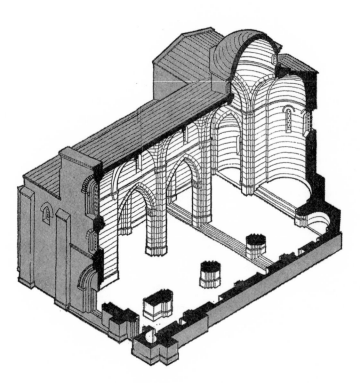

Architectural scheme of the Church
of St. Anne

The Dome of the Rock with the edicule of the Ascension of Mohammed, probably
the crusading baptistery

THE TEMPLE
AREA

Opposite page:
Doorway to the
Calvary. Slab in
high relief and
fragment of a
voussoir from the
Museum of the
Greek Patriarchate
of Jerusalem

If the Hospitallers, using the neighbouring mason's yard of the Holy Sepulchre, were thus provided, the rival Order of the Temple had equal, though different, talents at their disposal. Originally entrusted to Augustinian canons, the Temple area, much extended by Herod the Great, the platform on which stood the Temple and on which stands the Dome of the Rock, passed in the mid-twelfth century to the knights who took their name from it. The Dome itself, visible from so many points of the city, one of the world's great masterpieces, was built by the caliph ʿAbd-al-Malik ibn-Marwān, between 685 and 691. In conception it was a Byzantine building, a great dome set on an octagon, decorated with mosaics and Kufic inscriptions. The outer covering of Persian tiles, replacing mosaic patterns, was given to it by Sulaimān the Magnificent in 1561. To the crusaders, whatever its architectural style, it was *Templum Domini,* and the sacred rock that it covered, and that was associated with Abraham's sacrifice, Jacob's dream, and David's threshing floor, was in all probability the actual site of the Temple altar. About 1142 (William of Tyre, our authority, is not precise about the date) it had been re-dedicated as a Christian church. The naked rock, sacred alike to Christian and to Moslem, was covered over with marble pavement, and surrounded with a great iron grill, one of the wonders of medieval metal work, now removed, to the advantage of the building as a whole, but to the loss of its historical continuity. The mosaics, some of them dating back to the original construction and all notable examples of floral and arboreal patterns, were fortunately preserved, as were many of the Arab inscriptions. William of Tyre tried to decipher them, but, if he succeeded in doing so, he disregarded the anti-Trinitarian content of some of them. To these splendid works, the crusaders added mosaic or painted representations of the events of scripture specially connected with the site, and placed Latin texts *in great characters* round the inside of the Dome.

Throughout the platform, the Ḥaram al-Sharīf, small shrines were built with open arches and cupolas, modelled on the eighth-century Dome of the Chain that the crusaders found there. These now, with arcades filled in, still exist, and the edicule of the Ascension of Mohammed is probably the crusading baptistery. At the south end of the enclosure stood the al-Aqṣa Mosque. There had been a mosque here since the early days of the Conquest, and it was the place of general worship, whereas the Dome was, despite its size and magnificence, essentially a shrine. Constant rebuilding had, however, taken place, and the crusaders found it a triple-aisled basilica with a dome over the crossing. They thought it to be the Palace of Solomon and therefore a fitting residence for their kings, but it was eventually handed over to the Order of the Temple and the royal court moved to the Tower of David. The Templars' design for its conversion into a new church never seems to have been completed. Probably it was an adaptation of the existing building. The present façade, though closely influenced by Western style and likely enough the work of Christian builders, is dated by an Arab inscription to 1227, and must be part of the restorations begun by Saladin after the capture of the city in 1187. From then onwards, with a brief exception for the free-thinking emperor, Frederick II, the Ḥaram al-Sharīf was prohibited to Christians, and any found there had to profess Islam or die; *the Koran or the sword was the doom of any bold intruder within its sacred precincts.* It was not till the second half of the nineteenth century that there was any relaxation of this rule.

Inside the Dome, in the small edicules at the new Aqṣa mosque, on doorways and fountains, there was ample scope for the stone-carver's art. Figure sculpture, on this most sacred Islamic site, has not survived, but foliage ornament was acceptable to the Moslems, and, rebuilt into *mihrabs* or reading platforms, much survives, deeply cut leaves, bending back at the tips or twisting into circular terminals. The work is curiously distinctive and of the highest quality. Nowhere else has the Romanesque use of classical models been so completely absorbed into a new, accomplished style. One small free-standing cupola on the platform has capitals where the design is partially blocked out, partially

completed, partially Arab work. The Temple masons must have been at work on it when Saladin's siege and capture of the city brought their labours to a close. Elsewhere there are splendid finished examples. In the al-Aqṣa mosque there is a *dikkah* or reading platform, twelve feet by six in extent, made up of crusading columns, capitals, and friezes ingeniously fitted together. The number of the pieces show that there must have been much such work available, cornices or balustrades, possibly much of it carved but not yet in position. On an outside pulpit the same carving is displayed, and above a doorway in the mosque a splendid panel, framed in knotted columns, seems to be the side of some tomb catafalque. In the Dome of the Rock the doorway leading down to the cave beneath the rock has, or had till very recently, a tympanum with two curling acanthus sprays and a central branch ending in a cone. In the cave itself is a carved niche with acanthus whorls and linked columns, corresponding closely, as Strzygowski has pointed out, to the design of the tomb of Baldwin V in the Holy Sepulchre as drawn by Elzear Horn in the first half of the eighteenth century, a tomb destroyed, or at least dismembered, by the Greeks in 1809.[12] On the child king's death Guy of Lusignan seized the throne by the aid of the grand master of the Temple, and it would have been fitting enough that the tomb should have been ordered from the Templars' yard.

The coupled columns, linked by a series of knotted coils, which is such a distinguishing feature of the tomb design and the niche, is a not uncommon Byzantine formula, though generally limited to two loops. Thicker interwined columns are still to be found in the Temple area and a ninettenth-century photograph shows three such columns supporting blocked-in arches on the east of the Temple area. Originally an open arcade of these curiously devised supports must have been a prominent feature of the crusading plan. In the Mosque of the Serpents at Hamah similar linked columns are found, fourteenth-century work so that it is either an Arab formula or one that they absorbed into their repertory.

Niche in the Dome of the Rock

Tomb of Baldwin V, from a drawing of Elzear Horn.

19

The Ḥaram al-Sharīf has undergone constant alteration, and recently in the reconstructions, completed in 1964, following the damage done in the war with Israel, when the Dome was hit by a shell, there has been much displacement of crusading work, banished to the Ḥaram Museum or possibly destroyed. The church of the Holy Sepulchre has had greater vicissitudes, and has not yet received the long and careful restoration that has been given to the Dome of the Rock. Saladin allowed Christian entry to it, only it is said removing the bells from its tower, and some access was always permitted, though at times very grudgingly. Arab and Turkish rule claimed to be impartial among Christian sects and tolerated, no doubt with some malicious pleasure, their disputes and competing claims. The Latin Patriarchate came to be a title held *in partibus* and in the fourteenth century care of the Holy Places passed to the Custodia of Terra Santa of the Franciscan Order. So long years went by. Occasionally there were persecutions and martyrdoms. In 1719, protected by the military against mob violence, the Greeks and Latins carried out some urgent repairs and removed the two upper storeys of the bell tower which were in a dangerous state. Then in 1808 a fire broke out in one of the storerooms and rapidly spread, damaging the whole building. Restoration was carried out by the Greek Church in the following year, under the supervision of an architect from Mytilene, by name Comnenos. The columns, many of them calcined by the fire, were encased in piers filled with rubble, and walls were built between them. Many windows were blocked. The work was urgent and ungainly; it held the building together till in 1927 a severe earthquake brought new damage. The twelfth-century dome over the crusading crossing had to be demolished and a new one built, and in 1935 the Mandatory Government produced a detailed report on the state of the building. Since then the façade has been hidden by a network of supporting scaffolding. Now agreement has been reached between the three chief ecclesiastical authorites, Orthodox, Armenian, and Latin, and work is in progress which may not only preserve the building but restore it to a more worthy state.

Restored view of Great Cloister from the east.

Proposed restoration of cloisters and tower of the church of the Holy Sepulchre; from a drawing by G. Jeffrey.

Round Jerusalem a number of important churches marked the sacred sites without the walls. More exposed in times of war and disturbance, they survive for the main part as fragmentary ruins or as nineteenth-century rebuilding. In the valley of Kidron that separates the city from the Mount of Olives, the church of the Tomb of the Virgin still has its twelfth-century entrance doorway, though set in a façade that has lost its upper storey. Within, a flight of stairs leads down to a cruciform crypt, covered with a groined vault and built in well-cut stone. Here is the sarcophagus known as the Virgin's tomb, whose emptiness played a part in the twelfth-century debates as to the corporeal assumption. The church belonged to the Abbey of St. Mary of Jehoshaphat, founded by Godfrey de Bouillon and much patronized by Queen Melisend, whose tomb was in a niche half way down the staircase to the crypt. Traces of the monastic buildings were found when in 1937 a new sewer had to be driven through the site, bringing to light mosaic floors, fragments of wall frescoed in floral patterns, and the base of a large pier with engaged columns. The monastery was well endowed with lands and trading privileges in Sicily and southern Italy, and these excavations indicate that its buildings had an appropriate splendour. But when Saladin took the city, they were pulled down to provide building stone for the repair of the walls.

The monastery had also in its charge the grotto of the Agony and the church of Gethsemane, or of the Saviour. Built above Byzantine ruins the latter was a typical crusading church of nave and two aisles ending in three apses, now only known as an excavated ground plan. John of Würzburg described it in 1165: *there is a chapel with a grotto, where the sad and sleep-oppressed disciples waited, and where the Lord three times returned to them. The place where our Lord prayed is enclosed by a new church, called the church of St. Saviour: from its pavement stand out three stones, unworked, like small rocks, on which, it is said, Jesus three times knelt and prayed. The faithful kiss these stones and place their offerings there with the deepest veneration.*[13] It was not as simple a question as it seems in this account; the various sites of Gethsemane, those of Christ's prayer, the apostles' sleep, the betrayal, were to be much discussed. The grotto and the garden were both to have their advocates, and now rising above the traditional rock of the apostles are the seven Russian domes of the Church of St. Mary Magdalen built by the Czar Alexander III in 1888.

On the crest of Olivet were two churches, those of the Teaching of Christ, known as the Eleona, and of the Ascension. The Eleona was the third of the great Constantinian churches and was destroyed in 614 by the Persians. For a time it was replaced by two small shrines of the *Pater Noster* and *Credo*, commemorating Christ's teaching. Then in 1152 two Danish pilgrims left bequests for a larger church, of which nothing now stands and little is known. Here too there is considerable confusion as to the traditional sites, which, recalling as they do the teaching of Christ and his weeping over Jerusalem (*Dominus flevit*), are by the nature of the incidents hardly to be locally placed with any close accuracy.

The shrine of the Ascension still exists, a twelfth-century edicule, with well-preserved capitals, whose wind-swept leaves are the final development of the type used by the masons of the Holy Sepulchre. On one an owl spreads its wings, on another are two confronting griffons. This shrine was the central point of a circular Byzantine church, replaced in the twelfth century by an octagon, standing in a fortified enclosure.

At Bethany the tomb of Lazarus was the great object of pilgrimage. Here Melisend founded another monastery, of which today there are only fragmentary ruins, and a tower, still standing, that was part of the necessary defences of this outlying village. Between Bethany and Olivet, at Bethphage, a church, certainly with some twelfth-century work, marked the place of Martha and Mary's appeal to Christ, and also the start of the Palm Sunday procession, but the famous stone, painted with the raising of Lazarus and found in 1876, is certainly post-crusading work.

'AIN KARĪM AND OTHER SITES Elsewhere there was building activity: at 'Ain Karīm, where the crusaders enlarged a small Byzantine church in honour of the Visitation and the birthplace of the Baptist; at Nabi Samwil, the crusading abbey of Montjoie, where pilgrims had their first view of Jerusalem; on Mount Sion, where the crusaders rebuilt the Byzantine basilica, and where the room of the Last Supper, the Coenaculum, still exists, a vaulted Gothic upper chamber, most probably dating from 1239 to 1244, the period of Frederick II's peace. The church of Mount Sion underwent another rebuilding, when in 1898 the site was bought by the Kaiser, William II, and transformed into a rotunda, distantly modelled on that of Aachen. Now it is on the borders of the no-man's land between Israel and Jordan. Jerusalem, that has seen so much of the world's history, continues its unhappiness.

THE OLD CITY Within its circle of walls, it remains a predominantly medieval city, with narrow streets, some of them vaulted, with frequent steps on this uneven terrain. The houses and shops that line them are built from the local quarries and, through constant patching and rebuilding, retain an age-old frontage and elevation. The walls themselves as they exist date from the time of Sulaimān the Magnificent and from various inscriptions still in place seem to have been built in 1541–42. Basically their two-and-a-half-mile circuit must be that of Hadrian's wall, which in turn was re-used and adapted by the crusaders. Saladin repaired these defences, but in 1219 al-Mu'aẓẓam 'Isâ of Damascus dismantled them, fearing a Frankish reoccupation of the city. Partially restored by Frederick II, contrary to the terms of the treaty, the walls for the next three hundred years seem to have become steadily more and more ruinous. Sulaimān made of them a splendid example of Moslem building skill, with the Damascus Gate as their most grandiose feature.

The crusading citadel occupied the site of Herodian buildings by the Jaffa Gate, and Herodian masonry is still conspicuous in the Tower of David, the largest of the seven towers of this irregular enceinte enclosing a court divided into two wards by the old pre-Herodian Jewish wall. Here again there has been much rebuilding and much shifting of ground levels, but something of the strength of this, the central fortress of the crusades and dwelling of their kings, is still apparent.[14]

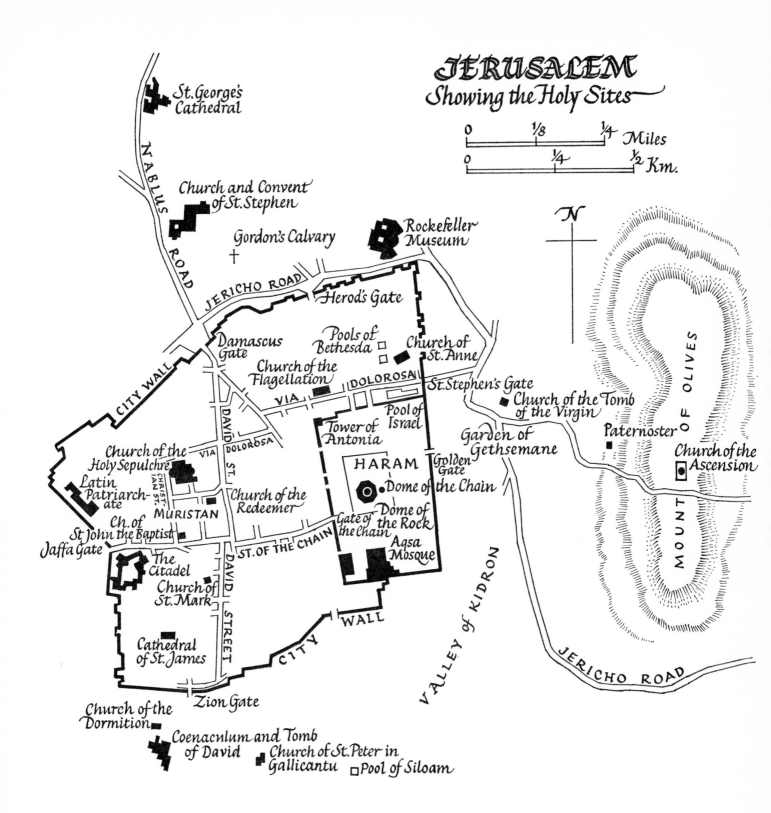

The Holy Sites of Jerusalem

The Dome of the Rock and Church of the Holy Sepulchre seen from Mount of Olives

# THE TRAVELLERS

PILGRIMAGE
AFTER THE
CRUSADING ERA

The loss of the crusading kingdom brought no cessation to pilgrimage. The very dangers and discomforts of the journey seemed to act as a challenge to the faithful, and the shrewd Venetians found it worth their while to provide frequent sailings for the pilgrim traffic. Many lost their lives by shipwreck or brigandage; some of the less discreet found martyrdom; but it is extraordinary how in the fourteenth century European Christians, generally now in Arab costume, wandered through the Near East from Cairo to Baghdad.

PILGRIMS'
DRAWINGS

In the fifteenth century, with the new realism in Western art, some of these pilgrims began to draw, or have drawn for them, things that they had seen. In the Hours of René of Anjou (British Museum, MS. Egerton 1070), painted c. 1436, there is an elaborate representation of the Church of the Holy Sepulchre with beyond it the Dome of the Rock. Much of the detail is correct, though the tall belfry, with its open arcades, is not only pure fantasy but structurally impossible. Another manuscript (Bibl. Nat. MS. fr. 64) has a closer rendering, and in the copy of the *Voyage d'outre-mer* of Bertrandon de la Broquière (Bibl. Nat. MS. 9087), written and illustrated for Philip the Good of Burgundy in 1453, there is a view of Jerusalem, which, though fanciful enough, is clearly based on memories of what Bertrandon or some other travellers had actually seen. Bertrandon was a new type of traveller. He was sent, as had been Ghillebert de Lannoy twelve years previously, by Philip of Burgundy to write a report on political conditions in the Near East, and he opens his account with the statement that it was written *to induce and attract the hearts of noble men who wish to see the world*. Unfortunately in Jerusalem he was so pre-occupied with *the customary pilgrimages* that he gives none of the details about its buildings and their condition that later in his journey he records of Constantinople.

It is with the woodcuts of Erhard Rewich of Utrecht, illustrating the account of the journey of Bernhard von Breydenbach published in 1486, that we have a more serious attempt at accurate delineation. The panoramas of Jerusalem and of Rhodes are invaluable documents, and his drawing of the Church of the Holy Sepulchre is an obviously careful piece of work with some real architectural understanding behind it. Whether Rewich himself had been to Palestine or whether he made his cuts from sketches by another hand is uncertain.[1] Probably von Breydenbach, a canon of Mainz whose tomb slab there shows a face of unusual sensitivity and distinction, provided the material. For almost a hundred years these woodcuts held the field, and frequent and unacknowledged use was made of them. Borrowings from them appear in some of Carpaccio's backgrounds, and the ships drawn by Rewich in the harbours of Rhodes and Modon reappear unexpectedly in the Basle edition of Columbus's *Epistola de insulis nuper repertis*. Then in 1585 a Belgian pilgrim, Johann Zvatlart, more generally known as Giovanni Zuallardo, provided in his *Devotissimo Viaggio di Gierusalemme* a more scientific rendering of the buildings, and also a series of drawings of towns such as Jaffa and Ramla and of the mountainous country round Jerusalem, scenes that enjoyed much popularity and were freely used to illustrate the accounts of other travellers such as John Cotovicus of Utrecht (Antwerp 1619), George Sandys (London 1615), and even the magisterial work of Francesco Quaresmi, the Franciscan guardian of Mt. Sion, who in his *Historica, Theologica et Moralis Terrae Sanctae Elucidatio* (1625) noted many inscriptions, now disappeared, in the buildings on the sacred sites. Meanwhile, however, another Franciscan, Bernardino Amico, had published in 1609 some careful and accomplished drawings of the architecture of Jerusalem and Bethlehem, drawings which are the soundest basis for our knowledge of them at this period. The Franciscan Custodianship, established in the fourteenth century in the face

THE FRANCISCANS

Opposite page:
The Church of the
Holy Sepulchre
and the Dome of
the Rock from the
Book of Hours of
René of Anjou, MS
Egerton 1070, f. 5,
in the British
Museum

of many difficulties, maintained the Latin rite in several churches, took what care it could of the buildings, and provided accommodation for pilgrims. George Sandys in 1611 rather grudgingly writes of them: *Nor is it a little that they get by the resort of the Pilgrims of Christendom. For all that come must repair to their Covent, otherwise they shall be accused for spies, and suffer much trouble; the Roman Catholicks rewarding them out of devotion, and the rest out of courtesie; which, if short of their expectations, they will repine at as losers. We four, for eight days entertainment, bestowed little less among them than 100 Dollars; and yet they told us that we had hardly paid for what we had eaten. A costly rate for a Monastical diet. But the Turk is much more fierce upon them; awaiting all advantages that may give a colour to extortion. A little before our coming, a Turk being denied by a Frier of some trifle that he requested, gave himself such a blow upon the nose, that the blood gushed forth; and present exclaiming as if beaten by the other, complained to the Sanziack; for which Avania they were compelled to part with eight hundred Dollars. Brought much behind-hand, as they alledge, with such losses, they use oft to rehearse them as motives unto charity.*[2]

William Lithgow, a Scotsman, who came to Jerusalem three years later than Sandys, writes that the friars were very welcoming, only asking *that those who did not share their beliefs should not mock at their ceremonies.* This cannot have been altogether easy for William, whose fierce anti-papal feelings explode in his writings: *Now thou bottomless Gulf of Papisterie, here I forsake thee. No winter-blasting Furies of Satan's subtile stormes can make shippe-wracke of my faith on the stony shelfes of thy deceitful deepes.* The canniness of his nation comes out in his comments: *Going doune another narrow Lane, they pointed unto a house, and saide, heere Dives the rich glutton dwelt, who would not give to Lazarus the crummes of bread that fell from his Table; this I suspend, amongst many other things, for all hold it to be a Parable, and not a History; and although it were a Historie, who can demonstrat the particular place, Ierusalem having been so often transformed by alterations.*[3]

Whatever the occupations and credulities of the friars there is from the fifteenth century onwards a series of Franciscan writings recording researches on the sites in their charge, without which our knowledge of them would be meagre indeed, a tradition still maintained in the publications of the Franciscan Press in Jerusalem, though even such able scholars as Father Bagatti and Father Hoade cannot rival the contribution to archaeological studies of Jerusalem made by the Dominican École Biblique through their immensely learned and indefatigably productive representatives, Father Vincent and Father Abel.

SECULAR TRAVEL    The seventeenth century saw the growth of secular travel, in which new interests began to replace religious obligations. More old fashioned ventures, it is true, continued, such as the journey in 1651 of Jean Doubdan, Canon of St. Paul's at St. Denis, who modestly apologizes for writing about matters which it might be thought should be treated only by those *qui ont blanchy sur les lieux*, but whose book in 1661 went into a second edition, and was *enriched with cuts*, scenes where small figures enact the stages of the Passion but which cannot claim any great topographical accuracy. Corneille le Bruyn may stand for the new type of traveller. A strong supporter of the house of Orange, suspected for a time through a confusion of names as being involved in the assassination of John de Witt, this young Protestant nobleman, whom a portrait by Kneller shows to have been very personable in looks, thus describes his reasons for setting out in 1674 on travels that were to occupy him for twenty years. *Forasmuch as most Men are naturally subject to some certain Inclinations, which 'tis next to impossible for them to resist, especially when by reasons of their Youth they are not capable of making any serious Reflections; it was my Fate to perceive in my self, even in my tender Years, an insuperable Propension of Travelling into Foreign Parts. And whereas I was then but just entring upon the publick Theatre of the World, I did not consider the Difficulties and Dangers to which such an Undertaking might expose me. When I was come to some Years*

LE BRUYN

J. M. W. Turner: Storm over Sidon; after a sketch by Charles Barry

28

*of Discretion, I found there was nothing more requisite and advantageous for a Traveller, who would reap any Benefit from his Travels, than to be skill'd in the Art of Designing, that thereby he might imprint Things the more deeply into his Mind, and represent them before his Eyes as always present, which is the surest way of keeping him from forgetting what he has observ'd. Upon this I applied my self to Painting, and having made a Progress therein, so far as I thought necessary for my Purpose, I set upon putting it into Practice.*[4] Le Bruyn was a trained draftsman, working in the landscape style of the late seventeenth century, and the copper-plates from his drawings have a sense of atmosphere that is new in representation of the Holy Land. His roof-top or interior views of the Church of the Holy Sepulchre, his 'Church of St. John at Acre', of which nothing now remains, are not only of documentary value, but have an emotional response to these historic scenes. His narrative is largely supplemented from earlier writers, his drawings and their originality are his own, all the more remarkable because they had to be made *with all the Privacy imaginable.... The Turks being always suspicious, that when the Christians take the Draught of any of their Towns, it is upon no design but to do them a Prejudice.* The plates at once made their mark; when in 1703 the Oxford Press published Henry Maundrell's *A Journey from Aleppo to Jerusalem*, the publishers stated MAUNDRELL that they *thought a Piece so well writ, ought not to appear abroad without the usual and proper Ornament of Writings of this kind, variety of Sculptures; and it having been design'd by the Author for a supplement to Sandys, their resolution, at first, was to furnish it with such Cuts, as are wanting in Him; but le Brune being since publish'd, and in every ones hands, such only are here inserted, as are wanting in both.* Maundrell was a fellow of Exeter College, Oxford, who became chaplain to the Levant Company's factory at Aleppo, and his very readable book, which by 1732 had reached its fifth edition, was long to be a guide to travellers. When in 1824 the first volume of *The Modern Traveller* appeared, devoted to Palestine, Maundrell is described as *perhaps the most correct, and one of the most intelligent of travellers.* His interest in the land in which he was stationed was not however characteristic of the Aleppo Factory, where the merchants found it safer to lead as isolated a life as possible, mixing little with the inhabitants. Maundrell speaks well of them, as *Pious, Sober, Benevolent, devout in the Offices of Religion; in Conversation, innocently cheerful; given to no pleasures, but such as are honest and manly; to no Communications, but such as the nicest Ears need not be offended at.... I have never known a Society of young Gentlemen, whether in the City, or Country (I had almost said the University too) so well disposed in all points as this.*[5] Archaeology, however, seems rarely to have figured among their *honest and manly pleasures.*

A characteristic eighteenth-century traveller was Richard Pococke, who visited the Holy Land in POCOCKE 1738. Classical remains and biblical sites were his main interest, and he was a painstaking observer of them. He gives a plate of the Sepulchre and the Rotunda *taken from the common drawings of it,* and it seems in fact to be based on that of le Bruyn, though from a different angle. He often mentions medieval remains, but his grasp of architectural styles was limited. The cathedral at Tortosa, the Gothic gem of the crusading states, seemed to him probably a building of the sixth century. At Margat, which he describes in some detail, he reported the tradition that the castle was the work of the Franks, but adds *the truth is the whole or part of it was built under the Greek Emperors.* At Nazareth he tantalizingly states that *near the present church are some remains of a much larger, which seems by the architecture to be of the time of the empress Helena; for there remain several capitals, and bases of pillars, and other pieces of antient work, in a tolerable good taste; and over a door there is an old alt-relief of Judith, cutting off the head of Holofernes.*[6]

To Pococke, with his classical leanings, Baalbek was the climax of his travels, a place *where there are at present such remains, as may be said to exceed every thing of antiquity in that kind.* These huge, grandiose temples amazed him as they must have amazed the crusading raiders that from time to time penetrated thus far into Moslem territory. Pococke devoted several plates and a long chapter to them, but soon they were to have much fuller treatment. Robert Wood's two sumptuous folios, *The Ruins of Palmyra* (1753) and *The Ruins of Balbec* (1751) revealed to the West the scale and interest of these Syrian ruins, and had an immediate impact on architectural taste and on the aims and interest of Near Eastern travel.

Such interests, however, touched but incidentally, if at all, upon medieval matters. They are still dominant in two schemes carried out at the close of the century, though already a new catholicity of taste is becoming apparent. Inspired by the efforts of Wood and others two ambassadors at the Porte, facilitated in their task by diplomatic privileges, vied with one another in recording the antiquities of the Near East. The French ambassador, Count Choiseul-Gouffier, a forerunner of Elgin in pillaging the Parthenon, employed Louis François Casas, an experienced artist, whose *Voyage Pittoresque de la Syrie* appeared in 1799. Casas has a new feeling for ruins and the picturesque and his views of Sidon and Antioch give full play to their romantic associations. At the latter, much of the circuit of walls was still standing, as restored by Justinian after the great earthquake of 526 and the capture of the city by the Persians in 540. Some repairs were made after an earthquake in 976 and it was then that the citadel was built at the highest point of the circuit. These were defence works that had defied the crusading army for almost a year, from October 1097 to June 1098, and the Franks seem to have done little to modify their form. The wall was a single one, reinforced by rectangular projecting towers linked to the chemin-de-ronde, rising steeply and following the contours of the hill. On the west above the Gate of St. George there was a large polygonal tower, which seems to have been the main strong point of the Byzantine scheme. On the south a deep gully cuts the hillside, and this was blocked by a great wall of masonry, the Iron Gate, partially to close the access, partially to prevent floods from sweeping down into the town. Casas could still depict these walls as imposing monuments, and we owe to him our most vivid realization of the medieval town. Ibrāhīm Pasha in the 1830's quarried stones from them to build a barracks, and the destruction was completed by an earthquake in 1872, leaving only foundations visible, though the Iron Gate still stands. Among his other drawings he has left us one of himself arrested by Arabs while sketching at Homs.

Luigi Mayer, who worked for the British ambassador, Sir Robert Ainslie, was a more prosaic artist, whose views published in 1804, though drawn some fifteen years earlier, have, however, the advantage of being coloured aquatints as opposed to Casas' copper engravings, and are the first colour prints of Palestinian subjects.

The outbreak of war with France in 1793 produced a complicating factor in foreign travel, and in 1798 the French expedition to Egypt and its eventual defeat, with the capture of Alexandria by the British in 1801, immensely changed the whole position in the Near East. *These are favourable times,* wrote Dr. Edward Clarke, *for travellers in the Levant, when frigates are daily sailing in all directions, and the English name is so much respected.* He himself, accompanying a young and wealthy pupil, had travelled via Scandinavia and Russia to Constantinople, from there joining his brother, a naval captain, at Alexandria. An expedition was made to Syria and Palestine, and his drawings, where the buildings matter little and the scenery is the subject, are a new departure: Acre from the sea with the hills beyond, a distant view of Nazareth, the Sea of Galilee with the houses of Tiberias an incident in the foreground. Of the last he writes, in the new vein of the student of landscape: *It is by comparison alone that any due conception of the appearance it presents can be conveyed to the minds of those who have not seen it; and, speaking of it comparatively, it may be described as longer and finer than any of our Cumberland and Westmoreland lakes, although perhaps it yields in majesty to the stupendous features of Loch Lomond in Scotland. It does not possess the vastness of the Lake of Geneva, although it much resembles it in particular points of view. The Lake of Locarno in Italy comes nearest to it in point of picturesque beauty, although it is destitute of any thing similar to the islands by which that majestic piece of water is adorned. It is inferior in magnitude, and, perhaps, in the height of its surrounding mountains, to the Lake Asphaltites; but its broad and extended surface, covering the bottom of a profound valley, environed by lofty and precipitious eminences, added to the impression of a certain reverential awe under which every Christian pilgrim approaches it, give it a character of dignity unparalleled by any similar scenery.* Clarke was a courageous but sceptical traveller. At Sephoria (Saffūriyah) *the House of St. Anne presented us with the commencement of that superstitious trumpery, which for a long time has constituted the chief object of devotion and pilgrimage in the Holy Land.* He secured, however, three pictures *in the antient style,* lately found in cleaning out *an old vaulted lumber-room* in the church. These all had Arabic inscriptions and must have been icons of the local Christians. At Jerusalem the Franciscans won his approval by providing the English party with tea: *This pleasing and refreshing beverage was served every morning and evening while we remained, in large bowls, and we drank it out of pewter porringers. For this salutary gift the monks positively refused to accept our offers of compensation, at a time when a few drachms of any kind of tea could with difficulty be procured from the English ships in the Mediterranean, at the most enormous prices. Persons who have not travelled in these latitudes will perhaps not readily conceive the importance of such an acquisition. The exhausted traveller, reduced by continual fever, and worn by incessant toil, without a hope of any comfortable repose, experiences in this infusion the most cooling and balsamic virtues.* When, however, he came to the Church of the Holy Sepulchre, nothing could restrain his Protestant fervour, and he attacked with vigour the authenticity of its claims, urging that the site of Golgotha was on Mount Sion. His arguments for the new site received little assent. *If,* he wrote, *during an endeavour to remove existing prejudices, and to excite a due contempt for Monkish errors, the subject seem rather perplexed than elucidated, it is because, in the subversion of a fabric raised by Ignorance and Superstition, its parts must necessarily lie scattered and confused.*[7] He opened, however, a debate that was to be an active one from then onwards. Chateaubriand, as might be expected, states in 1812 the opposing view: *The first travellers were indeed happy; they were not obliged to enter into these difficult problems: firstly, because they found in their reading the Religion that never disputes with the truth; secondly, because everyone was persuaded that the only way of seeing a country as it is was to see it with its traditions and its memories, and it is in fact with the Bible and the Gospel in hand that the Holy Land should be visited. If one wishes to bring there a contentious and intriguing frame of mind, there is no need to seek it so far afield. What would one say of a man who, travelling through Greece and Italy, occupied himself only with contradicting Homer and Virgil? Yet that is how one travels today: our self-conceit makes us to wish to appear clever and only renders us arrogant.*[8]

The war in the Near East provided opportunities of travels to others more actively engaged in it than was Dr. Clarke. F. B. Spilsbury, a surgeon on H.M.S. *Le Tigre,* published in 1803 *Picturesque scenery of the Holy Land and Syria during the campaigns of 1799 and 1800:* the plates were aquatints, coloured stipple engravings and coloured soft grounds etchings, drawn by Edward Orme from Spilsbury's sketches *on the spot.* These pleasant views enjoyed some popularity and the book was re-issued in 1823, but they add little to our knowledge of the buildings. Captain Henry Light in his *Travels in Egypt, Nubia and Cyprus in the Year 1814,* undertaken during a period of leave from Malta, drew a view of Jerusalem from the terrace of the Franciscan convent, where all European visitors were accommodated. More important archaeologically were the travels of the Hon. Charles Irby and James Mangles, commanders in the Royal Navy, whose *Travels in Egypt, Nubia, Syria and Asia Minor in 1817 and 1818* were printed for private circulation in 1823. They were close and interested observers and attempted accurate descriptions of the places they visited. Anyone studying the architecture of Palestine and Syria will always be much indebted to them, though their assessments of dates and styles were limited by the general theories of the period. Amongst other sites they reached Palmyra and Petra, travelling in Arab dress. Native costume had hitherto been essential in all Arab countries. Now

SPILSBURY

LIGHT

IRBY AND
MANGLES

there was some relaxation: *the address and gallantry of Sir Sidney Smith at Acre,* wrote a visitor in 1817, *have procured for the English a degree of consideration not extended to the individuals of any other Christian community. I have frequently thrown off my Arabian cloak, and walked through different parts of the city in a light Smyrna hat and common hunting frock, without experiencing the slightest inconvenience.*[9]

BUCKINGHAM

An even more adventurous traveller was J. S. Buckingham, whose career was summed up as follows, when, in later years (1837), he was being introduced as speaker at the Banbury Mechanics Institute: *A sailor boy at nine years of age; a prisoner of war at ten; a mariner in youth and early manhood; then a merchant in foreign parts; afterwards a traveller for years; a resident in India, applying his talents in literary and political pursuits, and since following them up at home—storms, plagues, shipwreck, battle, imprisonment, hunger, thirst, nakedness and want were his frequent portion.*[10] He was, however, more interested in the habits and customs of the country, than its ancient remains, though he has something to say of them and vigorously rebuts Clarke's doubts about the Holy Sepulchre. *Through the greater part of the country I passed as a native of it, wearing the dress and speaking the language of the Arabs, and by these means commanding a free intercourse with the people in their most unguarded moments and opening sources of information which would otherwise have been inaccessible.* But in the remoter areas in which he delighted, there were still many obstacles to detailed research: *My journeys were often through countries, where writing, drawing, or minutely surveying any subject, would have been fatal; where we often travelled with our hands upon our swords, and our eyes keenly watching for secret plunderers, or more open enemies.*[11] At Jedda in 1814, Bucking-

BURCKHARDT

ham met a man as enterprising and more learned than himself, John Lewis Burckhardt, and discussed with him the possibility of joining a pilgrimage to Mecca, a feat which Burckhardt accomplished, with such perfection in his command of Arabic and Islamic lore that none of his fellow pilgrims suspected the presence of the first European to enter this forbidden city. Buckingham was at this time too ill to attempt the journey, and he lacked Burckhardt's great learning. It is probably fortunate that he never tried this dangerous enterprise. Burckhardt's *Travels in Syria and the Holy Land* published posthumously in 1822 covers some little visited areas, but he was an Arabist and a classic, and medieval remains receive little comment.

BARRY

A less ambitious traveller was Charles Barry, later to be celebrated as the architect of the Houses of Parliament, who as a young man of twenty-four was taken to Palestine by a wealthy patron, to make sketches on the spot. Barry's drawings were not published, but they were used as the basis for more

TURNER

elaborate work by other artists.[12] J. M. W. Turner for instance painted from them his *Sunrise over Nazareth* and his *Storm over Sidon,* which were engraved for John Murray's *Illustrations of the Bible,* published in 1834. Some forty years earlier, the publisher Macklin had undertaken a great illustrated bible, and the leading English artists of the day, even the great Reynolds himself, had contributed 'historical paintings' to it, dramatic scenes in what passed then for appropriate costume. By 1834 tastes and interests had drastically changed, and Murray's *Illustrations* aimed at *a series of matter of fact views of places mentioned in the Bible as they now exist.* It was hard for Turner to be matter-of-fact. His castle-crowned peninsula at Sidon, with the whirling storm above, is well in the centre of the new romanticism. But the claims of the publishers were for topographical exactitude, for the real as opposed to the imagined. *Independently of the interesting associations connected with*

> ' *Those holy fields*
> *Over whose acres walk'd those blessed feet*
> *Which fourteen hundred years ago were nail'd*
> *For our advantage, on the bitter cross*' (Shakespeare),

David Roberts: The Church of the Holy Sepulchre

*the Land of Palestine, as it is well known, abounds in scenes of the most picturesque beauty. Syria comprehends the snowy heights of Lebanon and the majestic ruins of Tadmor and Baalbec. The gigantic temples of Egypt, the desolate plains of Babylon and Nineveh, the ruined cities of Idumea, Moab, and Ammon, and the rocky solitudes of Mount Sinai—all afford subjects most admirably adapted to the artist's pencil. But, notwithstanding the surpassing interest which attaches itself to Scripture localities,* very few, *even of the most remarkable places* mentioned in the Bible, *have ever been delineated. The few wretched engravings which occur in books of Travels convey a very inadequate idea of the places which they are intended to represent. By the kindness of the distinguished Travellers whose names are prefixed—aided by the obliging and zealous assistance of Captain Mangles, R.N. (who, though no draughtsman himself, has so admirably portrayed with his pen the scenery of the Holy Land)—the Proprietor of the* Illustration of the Bible *is enabled to supply this deficiency: these gentlemen having most liberally afforded the use of nearly Three Hundred Original Sketches, made by them during their travels in the East, from which selections will be made. No pains or expense have been spared in procuring from the most eminent artists, drawings and engravings which should combine the utmost excellence of art, with the most exact and faithful adherence to the original sketches.*

Acre, at that time once more the chief centre of Palestinian power, was between 1804 and 1819 under the comparatively enlightened rule of Sulaimān Pasha, and this, added to English prestige, facilitated the movement of travellers, though from time to time one or two fell victim to roving brigands. Under Sulaimān's successor, ʿAbdullāh, the Greek War of Independence roused local feeling against Christians and Westerners, and conditions of travel in the twenties became much more uncertain. The French traveller and archaeologist, Léon de Laborde, writes of those days: *In our days an exploration of this kind is a promenade; in 1827, it was an adventure; Colonel Boutin, Seetzen, Hennicker had recently been assassinated, victims of their devotion to knowledge; Mohammed Aly had not made Turkish haughtiness to bend nor disciplined Arab violence; the black hat or the status of the French, far from being a respected safeguard, roused all the worst sentiments of fanaticism.*[13] DE LABORDE

It was in 1831 that Mohammed ʿAli, having secured virtual independence in Egypt, intervened in Syria. He had sent a force under his son, Ibrāhīm, to assist the Turks in the Greek war, and, when the campaign there was stopped by the intervention of the Western powers, he claimed Syria from the Sultan as compensation for his son. This being refused, Ibrāhīm laid siege to Acre in 1831, and for the next nine years was practically in control of Palestine and much of Syria, a period of Westernizing policy, where travellers were encouraged (Mohammed ʿAli even knew of and approved Burckhardt's journey to Mecca), and of much destruction of ancient buildings to further Ibrāhīm's schemes of refortification. The Rev. Vere Monro, whose book (1835) is significantly called *A Summer Ramble in Syria*, writes: That whereas at the gate of Damascus foreigners used to be disarmed and not admitted except in Turkish dress, they could now enter freely, and he rode through the town wearing his tall hat and preceded by a muleteer crying out 'Mohammed Ali Pacha'. RULE OF MOHAMMED ʿALI 1831–40

Amongst the travellers of the thirties were John Carne and William Bartlett, who combined in 1836 to publish *Views of Syria, the Holy Land, Asia Minor, etc.* John Carne had travelled in the Near East in the troubled days of the Greek War, hearing from survivors of the horrors of the massacre at Chios, that so much held Western imagination. William Bartlett was a pupil of John Britton and had worked for him on his *Picturesque Antiquities of English Cities.* He was, therefore, trained in that recording of medieval buildings which was so characteristic an activity of early romanticism. Bartlett brought this new interest with him to Palestine. The castles at Tripoli, Sidon, Baghrās, Beirut, the walls of Antioch and Acre, the interiors of the Church of the Holy Sepulchre and the cathedral at Tortosa are amongst his illustrations. Twice he returned to Palestine in 1842 and in 1853, the latter period being one marked by many tensions in Jerusalem over the growing disputes between Russia and Turkey, that were to lead to the Crimean War. A friend of Bartlett's, F. Catherwood, was the first European since the crusading period who was able to examine in some detail the Dome of the Rock and the Ḥaram. In 1833 he had been making drawings from the roof of the governor's house, the usual view-point for foreigners. *Having so often looked upon the interesting buildings, which now occupy this celebrated spot, I feel irresistibly urged to make an attempt to explore them. I had heard that for merely entering the outer court, without venturing within the mosque, several unfortunate Franks have been put to death, and you may therefore conceive the attempt was somewhat rash. However, there were many circumstances in my favour; it was the period of the rule of Mehemet Ali in Syria, and the governor of Jerusalem, with whom I was on good terms, was a latitudinarian as to Mahometanism, like most of the pasha's officers. I had brought with me a strong firman, expressly naming me as an engineer in the service of his Highness. I had long adopted the usual dress of an Egyptian officer, and was accompanied by a servant possessed of great courage and assurance, and who, coming from Egypt, held the 'canaille' of Jerusalem in the extreme of contempt. This man had strongly urged me to the experiment; and at last, notwithstanding the remonstrances of my friends, I entered the area one morning, with an indifferent air and proceeded to survey, but not too curiously, the many objects of interest it presents.* The success of the first attempt encouraged Catherwood to set up his camera lucida and begin to make a drawing: this at once led to trouble from which he was only extricated by the timely arrival of the governor, who, assuming or pretending to assume, that these proceedings had the authorization of Mohammed 'Ali, introduced Catherwood to the mosque authorities as an engineer sent on a special mission, and secured him six weeks of undisturbed investigation of the two mosques and their precincts, including even the small chamber beneath the sacred rock.[14] Bartlett had much hoped to be able to visit the Ḥaram, but it was still prohibited territory, though several Europeans had risked entry in disguise. The following year, 1854, an engineer, Dr. Barclay, was invited to give a report on the buildings and was given every facility for visiting them. The Marquis de Vogüé, in 1853 to 1854, when he was in Jerusalem was, however, unable to obtain access: when he returned in 1862, he found a changed situation: *All-powerful bakshish has forced the doors... the formalities were completed... and we took possession, in the name of archaeology, of this enclosure so long closed to serious investigations.*[15]

More important than Bartlett as an artist, and equally interested in architecture, was David Roberts, who, having already made a name for himself with lithographs of Spanish subjects, travelled in Egypt and Palestine in 1838 and 1839. Armed with a firman from Mohammed Ali, he was able to sketch with some freedom, even in some of the mosques. His aim was, needless to say, to illustrate biblical history, but his interests were architectural and his drawings of the Holy Land comprise a considerable number of medieval buildings. The popularity of his work increased the demand for visual accuracy.

WILKIE *Now that Syria is open,* wrote Sir David Wilkie in 1840, *and that steam-boat navigation is spreading crowds in all directions, may not a system of scripture painting be required corresponding, not to our ignorance, but to our improving knowledge of Syria.... It is a fancy or belief that the art of our time and of our British people may reap some benefit, that has induced me to undertake this journey. It is to see, to inquire, and to judge, not whether I can, but whether those who are younger, or with far higher attainments and powers, may not in future be required, in the advance and spread of our knowledge, to refer at once to the localities of Scripture events, when the great work is to be essayed of representing Scripture history. Great as the assistance, I might say the inspiration, which the art of painting has derived from the illustration of Christianity, and great as the talent and genius have been this high walk of art has called into being, yet it is remarkable that none of the great painters to whom the world has hitherto looked for the visible appearance of Scripture scenes and feelings have ever visited the Holy Land. What we therefore so much admire in the great masters, must be taken from their own idea, or from secondary information. In this, though Paul Veronese, Titian, Giorgione, and Sebastian del Piombo, all Venetians, have by commerce, and immediate intercourse with the Levant, succeeded in giving in their work a nearer verisimilitude to an Eastern people; yet who is there who cannot imagine that such minds as Raphael and Lionardo da Vinci, great as they are, might not have derived a help had they dwelt and studied in the same land which Moses and the Prophets, the Evangelists and Apostles, have so powerfully and graphically described, and which they would have described in vain to the conviction of their readers, but as witnesses and participators in the events which form the subjects of their sacred writings?*[16] Syria was to prove less open than Wilkie anticipated. His arrival at Constantinople coincided with yet another bombardment of Acre, this time by a combined British, Austrian, and Turkish fleet. The Western powers had finally decided that the growing power of Egypt must be curbed and Ibrāhīm was driven from Palestine. Turkish rule, often ineffectual, returned and travel was to become again a more perilous business.

Wilkie brought from the Holy Land only sketches, and, dying on the return journey, had no chance to elaborate them into finished paintings. Fourteen years later Holman Hunt set out on a similar quest, inspired by the very strong desire *to make more tangible Jesus Christ's history and teaching*. The artists were leading the way in a demand for more accuracy. The archaeologists were bound to second them.

In 1841, at the instigation of King Friedrich Wilhelm IV of Prussia, a Protestant bishopric was set up in Jerusalem on the basis of a concordat (eventually dissolved in 1886) between the Anglican and Lutheran churches. It was a scheme that was never very clearly worked out, and which met with passionate opposition from the gathering forces of the Oxford Movement. It was one of the blows, Newman wrote later, that finally shattered his faith in the Anglican Church. But when the first bishop, Michael Solomon Alexander, a converted rabbi of Eastern European extraction, was appointed, he brought with him as chaplain a young fellow of King's College, Cambridge, George Williams, who at once interested himself in local antiquities. In 1845 he published *The Holy City: Historical, Topographical and Antiquarian Notices of Jerusalem,* which was to remain the fullest treatment of the subject until the magisterial work of the two Dominican fathers, Vincent and Abel, began to appear in 1914. Williams was an outspoken critic of other writers, and in particular of Dr. Edward Robinson, a learned American, who in his *Biblical Researches in Palestine* (1841) had denounced as inadequate the traditional evidence for the sites of Calvary and the Sepulchre. Williams' defence of their authenticity at once provoked further theorizing. In particular James Fergusson, the gifted but opionated architectural historian, replied with *An Essay on the Ancient Topography of Jerusalem* (1847), in which he claimed that the Dome of the Rock was the actual church erected by Constantine over the sepulchre. This eccentric view could hardly gain much assent, but Fergusson's persistent advocacy of it served to prolong the general controversy, which was followed with close attention in Germany, where almost simultaneously with Williams' book the Prussian Consul in Jerusalem, Dr. Schultz, had begun to publish the results of his researches. *The Holy City* is illustrated by lithographs from drawings made by the Rev. W. F. Witts, some of which are of considerable architectural interest; but of greater importance is a section contributed by Robert Willis on *The Architectural History of the Church of the Holy Sepulchre.* Willis, who held the chair of Applied Mathematics at Cambridge, had since 1835 been publishing important books and papers on medieval architecture, many of which are still authoritative and will always be held in respect by all later workers in this field. He never visited Jerusalem, but, using the notes and plans of others, and older documents, he produced a long essay which remains the basic discussion of the subject.

Not least among the travellers who took advantage of the comparative peacefulness of the thirties was Joseph-François Michaud. The foundations of the modern study of crusading history had been laid by Friedrich Wilken, whose first volume of the *Geschichte der Kreuzzüge* appeared in 1807. The first volume of Michaud's *Histoire* followed in 1812. It was a subject well suited to his rich, fluent, and

THE JERUSALEM BISHOPRIC

WILLIAMS AND OTHERS

WILLIS

MICHAUD

picturesque style, and his work soon interested and delighted many readers. In the preface to the 5th edition (1838), Michaud wrote: *Twenty-five years ago the greater part of the regions traversed by the Crusaders was almost unknown. Learning, fully occupied by research into the traces of antiquity, had forgotten those of the Middle Ages. The route of the ten thousand, the places made illustrious by the victories of Alexander, these were well known: but in this Asia Minor, which was the tomb of a million Crusaders, in these countries where the pilgrims of the West had met so many difficulties, so many misfortunes, and fought, not without glory, so many combats, we had no other guides than our old chroniclers, which almost never described the localities or gave only a confused idea of them. Without entering here into any detail, it is easy to judge of the information needed, of all that remained to be known to complete the history of these great movements of peoples, of these gigantic events which began in Europe and went to their final achievement in the East. I had, as I have said, never lacked clear ideas as to the events that had happened in the West; but for what had taken place under skies and in countries unknown, I was full of doubts. This great gap in my work has for many years tormented me and my conscience as a historian was quieted only when I have been able to follow the pilgrims of the Cross into the East. After having visited all the lands known to the Crusaders, I have still more realized what was lacking when I wrote my book. What seemed doubtful and obscure in the chroniclers has become clear to me: there are events of which I have become as it were an eyewitness; I have found a new facility in describing the sieges, the battles. I have better appreciated the heroism of the Crusaders, and explained to myself their perils, their misfortunes and their reverses.*[17]

Echoes of Michaud's theme, the neglect of the medieval inheritance, can be heard in the writings of DE VOGÜÉ another Frenchman. The Marquis Melchior de Vogüé spent the years 1853 and 1854 travelling in the Near East, and in 1860 published his pioneer volume *Les églises de la Terre Sainte*.

*One subject of interest had especially struck me: it was the abundance of the monuments of the crusading epoch, and their importance for the history of religious art in the West; it was the architectural role played by the crusaders in the Holy Land and particularly in Jerusalem, a role considerable, neglected and even unrecognized by the great part of modern travellers. There was in this, after the cares given to the sacred memories of the town and to the venerable debris of antiquity, a study to be made that seemed to me new and interesting... to determine the part played by the crusades in this architectural movement, to rediscover the buildings of this glorious epoch... to study them, above all to plan them, in order to provide some serious documents of study, and to aid in the solution of a much argued question, that of the influence exercised by these expeditions to the East on the development of our national architecture.*

It is the statement of a problem that was long to remain a dominant one in such studies, the true French preoccupation with their own nation and its artistic influences. The Marquis, who spent little more than five weeks in Jerusalem, had no time for a study that would be profound by modern standards, but he had Willis's brilliant account as his acknowledged guide for the Church of the Holy Sepulchre, and sound archaeological training as his own asset. His book is a remarkable achievement, and its value is much increased by the drawings in it. The frontispiece, de Vogüé's drawing of the south façade of the Church of the Holy Sepulchre, remains the most satisfactory rendering of the subject. The ecclesiastical art of the crusading kingdom had been revealed. There remained the re-discovery of their castles, which necessity made their most inventive achievement.

In the same year as de Vogüé's study of the churches appeared a book that had a different but great FRITH significance for architectural research, Francis Frith's *Egypt, Sinai, and Palestine* illustrated with photographs. *In a smothering little tent... with my collodion fizzing... it is truly marvellous that the results should be presentable at all.* But results there were; and the whole visual approach to the Holy Land was changed.

Krak des Chevaliers, distant view

# THE CASTLES

Biblical association or classical remains were up to the early nineteenth century the dominant themes. The great castles with which the crusaders had sought to control their uneasy dominions received little comment and were seldom visited. Some medieval pilgrims were impressed by them, and realized that they had prestigious beauty as well as defensive strength. Wilbrand of Oldenburg, Bishop of Utrecht, in particular, as befitted his knightly lineage, noted their fair fortitude[1] *(pulchra fortitudo )*, a phrase that he applies, when he visited it in 1212, to the Templars' castle at Tortosa, *crowned with eleven towers as with a diadem of precious stones, nor is it to be wondered at that the twelfth is lacking, since that tower, which the King of France built for the support of the land supplies the lack of it by its fair fortitude.*[1] Nothing is known of a grant by a king of France, but Philip Augustus may well have sent some contribution to the Templars, who had been installed there in 1183, and the tower in question was probably the great keep, built with the large and splendid masonry that so often was taken from classical ruins. Wilbrand also had much to say of Margat, occupied since 1186 by the rival order of the Hospital, *a large and very strong castle, fortified with a double wall, showing many towers, which seem rather to sustain the sky than to provide defence.* But such expressions of admiration are rare. Military experts must have studied with interest the crusading developments in fortification, but no record of their observations has come down to us.

It was the travellers of the early nineteenth century who found the castles appropriate and picturesque adjuncts of the scene. Even then the finest of them were little visited. Saone and Krak des Chevaliers lay off the main routes, and had no classical remains to attract exploring connoisseurs. Léon de Laborde visited the latter in 1827 and wondered at its nostalgic Gothic style: *One of the finest fortifications that can be seen. Surrounded by a wide ditch, reinforced by a wall flanked with towers and bastions, it presented, within, stairways, vast halls and numerous chambers, of which the construction, strong and skilful, rouses astonishment, while at the same time the Gothic style, everywhere apparent, charms the European traveller, happy to meet in this type of architecture with a memory of his forefathers.*[2] Margat was visible from the coastal road, but few travellers climbed the hill to give it closer inspection. *An hour north of the village of Markab is the great fortress of that name, a mile and a half in circumference, and crowning with its lofty and massive black walls and its two gigantic towers the summit of a steep and craggy off-shoot from the mountain range. The whole aspect of these half-ruined fortifications fills the mind with admiration and awe.*[3] De Saulcy in 1851 thought, *from a distance,* that the ruined fortress above Banyas seemed to belong to the period of the crusades, but, as he doubted whether there was a single ancient inscription there he *did not tarry to inquire.*[4] The castle of the sea at Sidon was a popular feature, and many artists drew it: Casas shows it in some detail; Bartlett more romantically; and Turner, basing his painting on a sketch made by Charles Barry, allows his romanticism full rein. Athlith, at the foot of Mount Carmel, was also on the coastal route, and there is a considerable account of it by Richard Pococke published as early as 1743, but Pococke though he recognized the *remains of a fine lofty church of ten sides, built in a light Gothic taste,* thought the castle itself, as he had also thought at Margat, *to have been built by the Greek emperors.*[5] Most picturesque of all, though rude work of uncertain origin, is the little castle of Msailha, perched on a rock rising from the valley that leads down to Botron, the old route from Tripoli to Beirut, which branched inland to avoid the rugged promontory of Ra's al-Shaq'ah. *About a league from the coast, the glen closes in, and the opening is barred by a rock 100 feet high, and 500 or 600 feet in circumference. This rock, whether shaped by nature or cut from the side of the adjoining mountain, is surmounted by a Gothic*

*See pages 46 and 47*

41

*castle, in a high state of preservation, but now the abode of the jackal and the eagle. Steps in the rock lead up, by successive ranges of terraces, to the highest platform, on which stands the donjon keep, with its ogeed windows and loopholes. Vegetation has fastened all over the castle, its battlements and towers; large sycamores have taken root in the halls, and spread their broad arms above the ruined roof; creeping plants hanging in huge festoons, ivy clinging to the windows and doors, and lichens everywhere clothing the stones, give this fine monument of the middle ages the appearance of a castle of moss and ivy.*[6]

GUILLAUME REY<br>
AND OTHERS

It was in 1871 that Guillaume Rey published his *Étude sur les Monuments de l'Architecture militaire des Croisés en Syrie et dans l'Ile de Chypre*. It was the first attempt to describe the castles in detail, to plan and measure them, and to trace their history. Little or no excavation could be carried out and in most cases the castles were inhabited by communities of peasants or brigands, little inclined to facilitate investigation. Rey must have possessed much tact as well as perseverance; his work is a great achievement and remains, if corrected in detail, the basis of all later study. His restoration of Krak des Chevaliers, drawn for him by Charles Sauvageot, fired the imagination of the West, already conditioned by the reconstructions of Viollet-le-Duc. In his concluding words Rey referred to the numerous researches that remained to be done, and hoped that his book might inspire someone to rescue from oblivion, while there was still time, this little known page of history. It was to Rey essentially French history, and it was the French who carried on his work, above all Paul Deschamps who, in 1925 and 1929, led archaeological missions to Syria accompanied by the architect François Anus. His work on Krak published in 1934 is the most exhaustive study that any medieval castle has received. It was followed by another journey in 1936, and his *Les Châteaux des Croisés en Terre Sainte* appeared in 1939. Meanwhile the English, who in the *Survey of Palestine* (1881–89) had dealt incidentally with various castles, began in 1932 the excavation of Athlith under the direction of C. N. Johns, an undertaking that was brought to a close by the outbreak of war and the end of the Mandate.

CONSTRUCTION<br>
OF CASTLES

The Byzantine fortifications seen by the crusaders on their route must have impressed them by their scale and planned control of the approaches to them. First in skill and magnitude were the walls of Constantinople. The triple line is composed of moat, outer terrace and wall, and inner terrace with the great wall dominated by its towers, round, square or polygonal, standing to a height of about 60 feet at intervals of approximately 180 feet, built of stone bonded with brick courses. There was in the West, where the walls of Rome were but a single line, nothing to equal this system of supporting defence works, with its variations in the angles covered and its solidity of construction. At Nicaea, the first major siege undertaken by the crusaders, there was a similar concentric system, much of which still stands today. Raymond of Aguilers describes it as *A town most strongly defended, both by nature and skill... encircled by walls that need fear no assault of men, nor shock of machines.*[7] Stephen of Chartres, writing back to his wife, Ada, the sister of William the Conqueror, tells of its *300 high towers and marvellous walls.*[8] The walls of Antioch, where the precipitous hillside made a single defence line all that was necessary or feasible, have already been described. In Syria the crusaders found smaller Byzantine fortifications, castles rather than town walls, and these were much simpler in form, following a quadrilateral plan with towers in the centre and at the corners of the walls. One of the towers was generally enlarged into a strong point. The crusaders followed this example in some of their lesser castles, such as Coliat (al-Qulaiʿah) in the north of the county of Tripoli, or at Darum in the very south of the kingdom, which William of Tyre describes as follows: *King Amalric had caused to be built on this site a fortress of moderate dimensions, covering scarcely more than a stone's throw of ground. It was square in form and at each corner was a tower, one of which was more massive and better fortified than the rest. There was neither moat nor barbican.*[9] When in 1170 Saladin laid siege to Darum, he penetrated the walls, but the besieged held out

42

in the strong point until a relieving force reached them. William of Tyre also describes the castles of Ibelin (Yabnâ) and of Blanchegarde (at-Tall aṣ-Ṣāfiyah), built by Fulk of Anjou in 1140–41 in order to guard against raids from Ascalon, as *adorned with four towers of suitable height,* which suggests quadrilaterals with four corner towers, though Rey, who saw ruins at Blanchegarde no longer extant, thought there may have been a central keep.

Eleventh-century castle building in the West was largely based on the fortified mound, protected in most cases with a wooden palisade, and a wall enclosing it or running down from it to form a bailey or court where refugees with their cattle could seek protection when there were raids on the district. Of stone castles, the greatest was perhaps the Conqueror's White Tower, commanding the eastern approach of London, though the keeps at Arques and Falaise in Normandy may well have preceded it. With its slightly projecting corner towers and its flat strengthening ribs, the Tower is the classic example of the Norman keep. Its original enceinte may have been a wooden fencework; certainly no trace of it remains in the later outer walls. A central keep was not unknown in Byzantine building, and Saone is a notable example of its use. The crusaders therefore found local reinforcement of their own Western tradition, and several of their early castles consist of a central keep in a quadrilateral enclosure. A typical example is Chastel-Rouge (Qalʿat Yaḥmur), close to Tortosa, where the square tower almost fills the small walled space, at two corners of which there are the remains of projecting towers. On a much larger scale, where the rectangular enclosure measures 530 × 400 feet, the castle of Belvoir (Kaukab al-Hawāʾ) was sited on the spur of a hill overlooking the Jordan valley as it opens from the Sea of Galilee, *situm in loco sublimi* as James of Vitry describes it. It was erected by the great castle builder, Fulk of Anjou, king of Jerusalem through his wife, Melisend, from 1131 to 1143, and was part of his scheme for the control of Galilee and the approaches from Damascus. Its defences on the east needed little artificial aid, but on the other three sides of its rectangle ditches were cut in the rock. At the four angles and in the centre of each side there were projecting rectangular towers faced with fine ashlar. Some uncertain remains suggest that there was a central keep, and there must have been buildings of some kind for the garrison and a chapel; but the outer walls were certainly its main strength. Saladin tried unsuccessfully to take it in 1182. *It seemed to us,* writes the author of *The Two Gardens, high as a star, the abode of the eagle.* In 1189 Saladin returned to the attack, pressing it on despite torrential rains. He announced its capture to Ṣaif-al Islām in the Yemen: *The most recent happening here is the taking of Kaukab, chief place of the Hospitallers, dwelling of those impious ones, residence of their chief, depot of their arms and provisions. This place situated at the junctions of routes, this observation post, where ways meet, being now conquered will henceforth be closed to the enemy. . . . When we came before Kaukab, the constellation that presides over winter showed itself with an escort of rains, the snows unrolled their carpet on the mountains. . . . God who knows good intentions aids their accomplishment.*[10] The change in frontiers deprived Belvoir of its importance. In the thirteenth century it was abandoned save for a few peasants. The walls crumbled and now only their foundations remain.

William of Tyre in his great *Historia rerum in partibus transmarinis gestarum* gives us many accounts of castle building and the reasons that prompted it. In particular he tells us of the ring of fortresses with which Fulk surrounded Ascalon, the strongly fortified outpost of Egypt that defied the crusaders until 1153. This is his account of the building of Ibelin. *About this time Fulk, king of Jerusalem, and the other princes of the kingdom, together with the lord patriarch and the prelates of the church felt the necessity of checking the insolent ravages of the people of Ascalon. In order to restrain them in some measure at least from overrunning the land freely, it was decided by common consent to build a fortress in the country near the city of Ramla and not far from Lydda, which is Diospolis. There was in that locality a hill slightly raised above the plain. Here, according to tradition, there had once been a city of the Philistines called Gath. Near here, about ten miles from Ascalon, and not far from the coast, was once another city belonging to that same people called Azot. The Christians responded as with one mind to the summons, and on the hill just mentioned, they built a fortress of very strong masonry with deep foundations and four towers. From the old buildings of which many vestiges remain to the present day, an abundant supply of stones was obtained. The wells of olden times which existed in large numbers in the vicinity of the ruined city also afforded an abundance of water, not only for use in the building operations, but also for the needs of man.*[11] Here are clearly stated some of the main factors: protection against raids; the normal four-tower, quadrilateral shape; the existence of wells; the re-using of stones from ruined buildings. As one of William's translators added *Chasteau abateiz est demi refez*, a castle pulled down is half remade. Ibelin (Yabnâ), which today has few traces of crusading building, guarded the coast road between Ascalon and Ramla, where it joined the road from Jaffa to Jerusalem, the main pilgrim route, so that it was part of the defence of this all important link between the capital and its nearest port. Writing of another castle, William states: *There, on the slope of the hill at the entrance to the plain, on the road leading to Lydda and from there to the sea, they built a fortress of solid masonry to ensure the safety of pilgrims passing along that route. In the narrow mountain pass, among defiles impossible to avoid, pilgrims were exposed to great danger. Here the people of Ascalon were accustomed to fall upon them suddenly. The work, when successfully accomplished, was called Castle Arnold. Thus, by the grace of God and also because of this fortress, the road became much safer and the journey of pilgrims to or from Jerusalem was rendered less perilous.* Castle Arnold (Bait Nubā) was to be the headquarters of Richard Cœur-de-Lion in his advance on Jerusalem, the point from which he turned back, *casting his surcoat before his eyes* so that he should not behold the Holy City which he could not rescue. It was again Divisional Headquarters in Allenby's advance in 1918. Its strategic importance has been well endorsed, but as with Ibelin little or nothing remains today of this crusading key point. William stresses another point when he writes of the building of Blanchegarde: *Those who dwelt in the surrounding country began to place great reliance on this castle as well as on the other strongholds, and a great many suburban places grew up around it. Numerous families established themselves there, and tillers of the fields as well. The whole district became much more secure, because the locality was occupied and a more abundant supply of food for the surrounding country was made possible.*

CASTLE ARNOLD

BLANCHEGARDE

There can be little doubt that to the crusading lords a prime function of a castle was, as in the West, to provide a focal point for the economic exploitation of the surrounding country. In a countryside mainly populated by an unreliable native population, the immigrants clustered for safety round some stronghold, and the number of castles was the result of their insecurity rather than the outcome of reasoned strategy. The Hospitallers in 1170 went so far as to complain of their grand master, Gilbert of Assailly, that he undertook the charge of castles and fortified places on the Turkish frontier *(in confinibus Turcorum)* and thereby burdened the Order with unnecessary expenses. Many of the castles in fact lie some way from main routes, built on hill sites that are excellent for defence, but centres from which any rapid deployment was difficult. Raiding parties constantly wandered far into crusading territory without meeting any organized opposition. Such forays, however, could, while the castles were still strongly manned, achieve no permanent hold. The existence of a castle, however placed, became in itself a factor in the strategic position.

Strangest of all in their use of natural defences were the cave fortresses at Tyron (Shaqīf Tīrūn) in the hills above one of the routes from Damascus to Sidon, and at Ḥabīs, above the Yarmuk to the south-east of the lake of Tiberias. The latter was an advanced post, in a country where a castle built by Baldwin I had been almost immediately destroyed. The caves, reached by narrow paths in the rock

44

The castle of Gibelet (Jubail)

face, partially natural, partially cut, required little expenditure and were almost impregnable. Tyron was lost to the Franks in 1165, but reoccupied for a time in 1250. Furnished with grain stores, cisterns and a water supply brought in pipes from a nearby spring, it was not easily starved out, and its vertiginous path of access was in places a matter of crawling on hands and knees under shelving rocks to reach entrances in the overhanging cliff.

Of the early castles, the most notable is that of Gibelet (Jubail). The town was captured by Raymond of St. Gilles in 1104, and the fortifications seem at first to have been based on a rectangular enclosure with corner towers. The square-headed arrow-slits in these walls and the segmental vaulting of their broad recesses belong to an early stage of the crusading settlement. Soon after, however, with slightly differing arrow-slits, a central keep was built, fifty-eight by seventy-two feet in plan. The site was that of ancient Byblos, and the castle rose upon layers of earlier civilizations. Old masonry was re-employed, and large blocks of stone, one measuring over sixteen feet by four, can still be seen in the walls of the keep. Marble columns were cut up and used as bonding, but this not altogether satisfactory practice seems more frequent in the Arab patching of the outer walls than in the actual crusading work. Saladin took the town and destroyed the enceinte, but when his men tried to level the tower, Burchard tells us, they *lost much sweat unavailingly*. This great rectangular tower has none of the flat buttress ribs that would be found in contemporary France or England: its solidity did not require such additions.

GIBELET
(JUBAIL)

45

The castle of Msailha

The castle of Msailha. Engraving after William Bartlett

Saone (Sahyūn) has little documented history until its capture by Saladin in July 1188. On one of the lesser routes from Latakia to Aleppo, in difficult country for any rapid manoeuvring, it was, like most of the castles, primarily important for its impregnability, but there could be no sure passage between the port at Latakia and the Orontes valley while this massive fortress remained secure in the intervening hills. The immense defensive nature of the site must always have been its main attraction, and probably from an early time there had been some fortifications on it. It was occupied by the Byzantine emperor, John Zimisces, in 975, and a considerable castle was built on the great rocky spur which projects from the hillside between two valleys. It was an area that remained in Greek hands, until Tancred occupied Latakia between 1106 and 1108. The first lord of Saone, Robert, was captured in battle in 1119, taken as a prisoner to Damascus and there executed. Nothing, save the barest mentions, is known of his successors, but there must have been an enterprising builder amongst them. The whole area of the spur was walled round, including the long narrow slope, where the walls show no trace of Byzantine building and which had been cut off by a ditch dividing the spur into two parts. Where the spur joins the hillside a far deeper and larger ditch had been built, and the Byzantine keep stands on slightly rising ground between the two ditches. Between this keep and the great ditch there seem to have been at least three walls, and possibly a fourth on the edge of the ditch, where the crusaders built their keep and a row of towers in splendid bossed masonry, and where there are some traces of Byzantine masonry in the lower stages of the walls. T. E. Lawrence writing to his mother from Aleppo in September 1909 describes it thus: *On the Monday I went from there to Sahyun, perhaps the finest castle I have seen in Syria: a splendid keep, of Semi-Norman style, perfect in all respects: towers galore: chapels; a bath (Arabian) and a Mosque: gates most original: and a rock-moat 50 feet across in one part, 90 feet in another, varying from 60–130 feet deep: there's a cutting for you! And in the centre had been left a slender needle of rock, to carry the middle of a drawbridge: it was I think the most sensational thing in castle-building I have seen: the hugely solid keep upstanding on the edge of the gigantic fosse. I wish I was a real artist.*[12] It is indeed a strange and overpowering spectacle. The ditch must originally be Byzantine work, for the nature of the site requires some barrier between the castle and the main

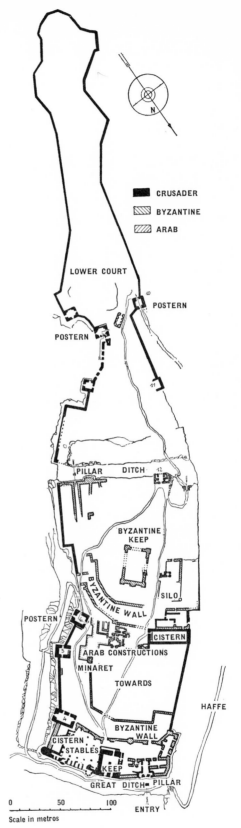

SAONE
(SAHYŪN)

Opposite page:
The ditch and rock
pillar at Saone

hill plateau, but the crusaders enlarged it, carving out on its sides rounded pilasters for some of the towers that are completely in their masonry. In the base of the towers are arrow-slits of a somewhat primitive type formed by leaving a gap between the stones. Inside the keep are a lower and upper chamber vaulted in stone, and in the wall beside it is a postern gate that could be reached by a drawbridge supported by the great needle pillar in the ditch. The entrance was on the south side, approached by a steep path running below the walls, with a right-angle turn inside the gateway, an early use of the bent entrance, which was probably based on Arab examples, as were the stone brattices, projecting on corbels, which also make one of their earliest crusading appearances. Saladin in his northern campaign after the taking of Jerusalem in 1187 bypassed Krak des Chevaliers and Margat, thinking them too strong to attack. On the coast Jabala and Latakia were the only two ports that surrendered to him, and for supplies he had to depend on the route through the Orontes valley. Saone blocked his most direct connexion, and he concentrated on re-

Round tower at Saone

ducing it. His secretary, Bahā᾽ ad-Dīn, has left us a vivid account of the siege operation. *When the Sultan departed from Laodicea, he marched upon Sahyun, on the 29th of Jomada I (27 July) surrounded the place with his army and set up six mangonels to play on the walls. Sahyun is a very inaccessible fortress, built on the steep slope of a mountain. It is protected by wide ravines of fearful depth; but on one side its only defence is an artificial trench about sixty cubits deep cut out of the rock. This fortress has three lines of ramparts, one round the precincts, another protecting the castle itself, and a third round the keep. On the summit of the keep rose a lofty turret, which I noticed had fallen to the ground when the Moslems drew near. Our soldiers hailed this as a good omen and felt certain of victory. The fortress was attacked very smartly from all sides at once, and al-Melek ez-Zaher, Lord of Aleppo, brought his mangonel into play. He had set it up opposite the stronghold, quite close to the wall, but on the other side of the ravine (Wadi). The stones hurled from this engine always reached their mark. The prince continued to play upon the place till he had made a breach in the wall large enough to enable the soldiers to climb the rampart. On Friday morning, the second day of the month Jomada II (29 July) the Sultan gave the command to assault, charging the men who had the management of the mangonels to shoot without ceasing. Then there arose mighty cries and a terrible noise, whilst our men shouted the tahlil and*

The castle of Saone from the west

*the takbir. An hour afterwards the Moslems had scaled the wall and burst into the courtyard. I saw our men seize the pots and eat the food that had just been cooked, without leaving off fighting. The people in the courtyard fled into the keep, leaving everything behind them, and all they abandoned was promptly given up to pillage. The besiegers surrounded the walls of the keep, and the garrison, thinking they would be annihilated, asked for quarter. As soon as this was reported to the Sultan, he granted their prayer and allowed them to depart with their household goods, but demanded a ransom of ten pieces of gold from each man, and five pieces from each woman; the children were to pay two.*[13] Almost certainly the point where the walls were breached was the north-east corner, where the ditch joins the natural gully between the spur and the opposite hillside, which here gives a commanding position to the besiegers. The walls at this point have obviously been much repaired and there is a nearly obliterated Arab inscription on them. Saone, after its capture by Saladin, was never again in Christian hands and had little history. A mosque was built, a small insignificant building, the walls were repaired, and the castle and neighbouring village were still in the nineteenth century of sufficient importance for Ibrāhīm Pasha to occupy it in his campaign. But there was little later building, and when Rey visited and roughly planned it in 1864 it had become an unknown site, partially overgrown, away from the main routes, unmentioned by travellers. It still today keeps something of this remoteness, its solitude rarely disturbed, its secrets not wholly explored.

Saone was a baronial castle. The great fortresses were mainly in the hands of the two military orders. The Templars at Tortosa successfully held out against Saladin: the Hospitaller fortress at Krak he left

KRAK DES
CHEVALIERS

51

unassailed. As the Parthenon is to Greek temples and Chartres to Gothic cathedrals, so is Krak des Chevaliers to medieval castles, the supreme example, one of the great buildings of all times. Ḥiṣn al-Akrād the Arabs called it, which the Franks turned into Le Crat and then, by some analogy with Kerak (fortress) into le Krak, or, from its tenure by the Hospitallers, Krak des Chevaliers. It has survived with remarkable completeness, and is one of the few crusading castles that has undergone systematic excavation and restoration by modern methods. Its history is a typical one. The original Arab fortress captured by Raymond of St. Gilles on his march south in 1099 was not finally occupied till 1110, as a dependency of the county of Tripoli. In 1142 Raymond II of Tripoli established the Hospitallers as the main bulwark of his small county. Without the appeal of the great religious sites, reinforced only from Provence where already heresy and anticlericalism were undermining crusading propaganda, the county of Tripoli lacked men and means and was the first area where the Order of the Hospital became a great landed power. Of this territory, Krak became the central garrison post. Its site illustrates all the various motives which underlie the castle building of the crusaders. Between the Jabal ʿAkkar, the northern point of the Lebanon range, and the Anṣārīyah mountains opens the Gap of Homs, the valley of the Nahr al-Kabīr between Homs and Tripoli. The castle does not block this passageway. It stands some eleven miles to the north of the main route on a steep hillside at a height of 2,300 feet, looking over a wide stretch of country but withdrawn from the main lines of attack. Its strategic function was essentially to supply a fighting force when required, or to act as a base for raids into Moslem country. *What think you of a town,* wrote Ibn-Jubair when he visited Homs, *that is only a few miles from Ḥiṣn al-Akrād, the stronghold of the enemy, where you can see their fires and whence each day the enemy may raid you on horseback.*[14] Ibn al-Athīr calls it *a bone in the throat of the Moslems:* Andrew of Hungary termed it *the key of the Christian lands:* it was a stronghold of immense importance and, though Saladin could pass it by on his northern campaign, there could be no permanent Moslem reconquest of these areas while it was in Christian hands. Its economic importance, however, seemed almost as great as its military to the crusading chroniclers. The wide valley below it was extremely fertile: *Rich in every kind of produce,* says the author of the *Gesta Francorum,* recounting the crusaders' first entry into it.

The earliest stage of the crusading work on the fortress cannot be accurately dated. Its first occupant, the William of Crat mentioned in Raymond's charter to the Hospital, may have been responsible for the undertaking. The plan was a walled courtyard with vaulted compartments built along the inner wall and opening on a central court. There were two entries, one at right angles in a projecting tower on the north-west face, possibly built on Arab foundations, the other a direct entrance on the east between two square towers. There were square towers also at the corners of the south face and in the west wall. The stones employed, brought from a local quarry, were drafted with a chisel and bossed. An earthquake of 1170 seems to have damaged the buildings severely. Abū-Shāmah tells us that *not one of its walls was left standing.* This is clearly an exaggeration, but it is probable that the chapel was rebuilt at this time, for in style it is close to that of Margat, built after the Hospitallers acquired it in 1186. Repairs must certainly have been fully carried out by 1188, when Saladin on his march north decided not to attack it. Krak remained one of the inviolate fortresses of this great crisis of the Crusades; as such it took a new prominence in the crusading counter-attack. The conversion, however, from a simple fortified courtyard to a highly developed system of concentric defences must have been spread over a considerable period. The first step was the building of the new outer enceinte. At the narrowest point, on the north, the gap between the two enceintes is about 52 feet; on the south it widened to 75 feet. At regular intervals along the walls (the west front provides a well-preserved stretch of this stage of the construction) were projecting semicircular towers; inside they had rectangular, vaulted halls on

Krak des Chevaliers from the south-west

the ground level, provided with three loopholes, one in the centre of the projection, one at each junction of the tower and wall, commanding the base of the wall on either side. Towers and walls were crowned with merlons, and the chemin-de-ronde was supported on a vaulted passage from which opened loopholes and stone brattices. The arrangement to secure the widest field of fire by alignment of the loopholes is carefully worked out, and, whereas on the earlier inner enceinte the loopholes are straight slits, here they have a stirrup-shaped opening at their foot allowing of direct downward shooting at the base of the wall. On the other three sides of the outer enceinte there has been much rebuilding, and in places the defensive scheme has been altered by some new feature. The history of this rebuilding, partly Frank, partly Arab, is far from clear, but there does not appear to have been any deviation from the line of the circuit built in the last years of the twelfth century.

The building of this outer enceinte secured a large addition of accommodation, much needed in the position Krak now held as one of the main rallying points. It also permitted on the inner enceinte of considerable re-planning, which could be carried out behind a first line of defence. Along the inner west wall was built a great talus, continuing round the south-west corner and along the whole of the south front. On the west side this talus joins the old inner wall, and provides covering for a long vaulted passage. Whereas the earlier building stage used bossed stone work, the second uses smooth-faced stone, consequently the two periods are easily distinguishable. On the south front the talus and the wall and towers above it have been advanced some way beyond the original line so that the talus passageway here is entirely new work. The central tower of the inner west front, originally rectangular, was converted into a splendidly built semicircular tower (O), joined by some admirable stone-cutting to the talus; but it is the south front where three great towers rise from the glacis above all the rest of the castle, with along their foot a water-filled cistern, which is the most striking and unforgettable aspect of this noble building. The masonry, all smooth-cut stone, is work of the most capable kind: arrow slits, the round open gallery walk of the central tower, the angle turn of the whole scheme near its central point, all show architectural skill and military science of a high order. Much of the outer enceinte must have fallen in the siege for on the south it is now mainly Arab work, including an enlargement of the south-west corner tower (6) and a rounded glacis such as is found at Beaufort; the great square tower (7) built in the centre of the south outer wall is marked with Baybars' lion and an inscription stating that it was completed by Kalavun in 1285. The enceinte however retains its original scheme, and there can be no doubt that its layout, the outer wall overlooked and supported by the great south towers of the inner, was thought out as a whole. The original entry was a direct one through two rectangular towers (H) and a central guard room: to this was added in the building schemes of the late twelfth or early thirteenth century a long ramp, descending at right angles from the earlier entry and running south, then turning, at a point controlled by the projecting pentagonal south-east tower (M), and running north-east with a sharp bend through a guard tower and a complete right angle bend at the exit. The eastern wall of this part of the ramp and parts of the eastern outer enceinte are built in poor masonry, but with mason's marks that appear to be crusading, and suggest hasty repairs when funds were low and time short. Very similar work is found in a barbican protecting the postern in the north front, which has an inscription assigning its construction to Nicolas Lorgne, who is known to have been in command at Margat between 1250 and 1254, to have become marshal of the Order about 1269, grand preceptor in 1271, and grand master in 1278. No document dates his command of Krak

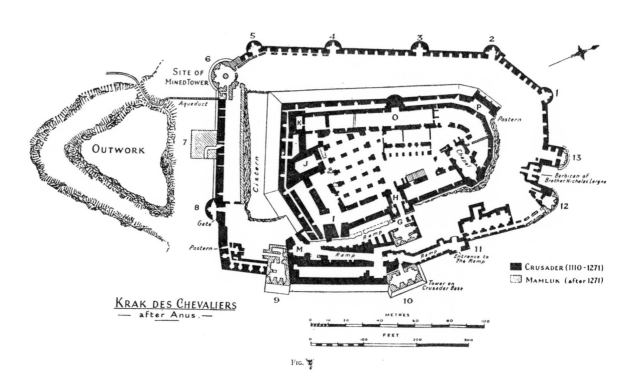

KRAK DES CHEVALIERS
— after Anus. —

CRUSADER (1110-1271)
MAMLUK (after 1271)

FIG.

54

but the likely period is approximately 1254 to 1269. In 1255 Alexander IV granted exemptions from the decime on the grounds of the cost of the upkeep of Krak, and this is probably the period of these somewhat poorly built parts of the outer defences. Baybars was already ravaging their territory and carrying off their dependent villagers; St. Louis' crusade had failed and it was time indeed to strengthen the defences of the entrances and build up any part of the walls that siege or earthquake had weakened.

One curious feature remains to be mentioned. At the north-west corner of the inner enceinte a rectangular tower (P) projects from the wall, protecting a small postern. The lower part of this tower is in the bossed masonry of the first building stage. It has a low talus above which rise three pointed arches, set in a wall slightly advanced so as to leave a space between it and the main curtain, thus forming three large machicolations, by which missiles from the top platform could be dropped onto the talus, rebounding against any enemy at the foot of the wall. This elaborate and surely somewhat ineffective arrangement was being tried out in France in the second half of the twelfth cen-

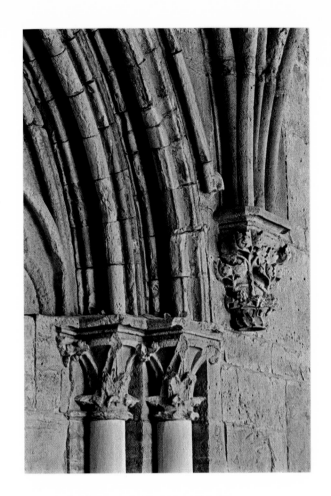

Detail of a doorway in Krak des Chevaliers

tury. Its vogue in Syria appears to have been a short one and in fact on the same tower the wall has been strengthened, reinforced by three blind arches above the machicolation openings, and crowned with a gallery of stone brattices, twelve in all. These have Frankish masons' marks, and may therefore be crusading work, though the use of continuous machicolations is characteristic of Arab fortification, and the great machicolated galleries of the southern outer enceinte are certainly Arab work, as opposed to the single or double stone brattices with which the crusaders generally contented themselves.

Within these varied and powerful defence works, the inner courtyard had buildings for more peaceful purposes. The western of the three great towers of the southern front (K) contained the room of the commandant, a round chamber with ribbed vaulting and some carefully cut decoration on the windows and capitals. Some adjustments suggest that this fine room had been made or re-modelled at a later date than the building of the tower, and its decoration suggests the second quarter of the thirteenth century, that period of hope when so many felt that Louis of France would redeem the Christian cause. The great southwork was clearly the habitation of the knights. It was carefully isolated by a gap of some ten feet from the raised esplanade above the buildings of the main court, and approach to it was only by a drawbridge. This seems intended more for internal defence against riots than for a final strongpoint. The brethren must often have been a minority in a very mixed garrison. Along the north and west of the court ran a great vaulted chamber, called by the French excavators the *salle de*

*120 mètres,* which contained the well, kitchens, latrines, and no doubt provided menial living quarters. On the north-east corner was the chapel, a severe and simple building with a single apse, 75 feet long by 30 broad, covered by a groined vault. Far more elegant was the loggia built opposite it, in front of the great hall or chapter house. Hall and loggia are alike covered with ribbed vaulting. The elaborate carving of consols and capitals, where the formal crocket is beginning to give place to natural leaves, and the fine tracery of the windows and the tympana of the doorways are in the happiest Gothic style of the thirties and forties. Apart from the cathedral of Tortosa, nothing of this period that survives in Syria can equal them in faultlessness of charm and elegance. This gallery must have provided a cool and sheltered resting place. On its walls are still inscribed in Gothic script a Latin jingle warning against pride. In this great massive fortress a military order must indeed have felt pride to be a temptation, till on an April day of 1271 Baybars' troops stormed the walls. But even then, with Krak for ever lost, the Hospitallers, wiser and perhaps humbler than their brother Order, had a great future before them and the buildings of Rhodes were to be a sequel to Qal'at al-Ḥiṣn.

FALL OF KRAK     It was on February 1271 that the Sultan Baybars encamped against Krak.[15] The dates and accounts of the siege vary in the different authorities, but it is clear that the village outside the walls was easily captured and that, probably on 21 March, the triangular outwork, traces of which still remain in front of the south face, was stormed. It was protected by ditches and walled with stone, for wood that could have made a palisade was certainly lacking. On 29 or 30 March a tower was mined and the invaders entered the outer enceinte, *massacring the Hospitallers, taking prisoner the mountaineers, but letting the villagers go free to keep up cultivation.* The tower is almost certainly the south-west tower of the outer wall (6), which here has been much rebuilt. Some of the knights still held out in the inner enceinte, the original twelfth-century castle with the later addition of the three towers of the south face. Baybars may well have hesitated when, breaking through the outer wall, he was faced with this most majestic of defence works, one that the slope of the ground reveals completely only from the outer ward. The Sultan according to some accounts sent the defenders a forged letter from Tripoli, enjoining them to surrender. Be that as it may, on 8 April the garrison received a safe conduct and handed over the castle.

LATER HISTORY     Krak remained a place of some importance, with its defences, if not much altered, carefully maintained. In the nineteenth century it was one of the strongholds never reduced by Ibrāhīm Pasha, but later it dwindled to a small village of some five hundred inhabitants. Under the French mandate a superintendent was appointed and, when in 1933, after much negotiation, it was ceded in perpetuity to France, the castle was cleared of its inhabitants and of the encumbrances they had inflicted on it. Empty and now purposeless it survives with something of the chill of a museum about it, but nowhere can the imagination have freer or less frustrated play.

MARGAT (AL-MARQAB)     On a spur of the Anṣārīyah mountains, overlooking the coast road between Tortosa and Latakia, the Hospitallers had their other great stronghold, the castle of Margat (al-Marqab, the water tower). Though a long stretch of the route is visible from the castle, it cannot be said to control it. To reach the castle is a two hours' climb and any force sent down to block the passage of an enemy force would be cut off by a steep line of retreat. The path leading to the fortress was, Ibn al-Athīr tells us, so narrow that two men could not pass each other on it. Saladin did not attack it on his northern campaign, but marched below it unhindered by the garrison, even though the Sicilian admiral, Margaritone, with his

Opposite page: Courtyard and loggia in Krak des Chevaliers

The castle of Baghrâs. See page 80

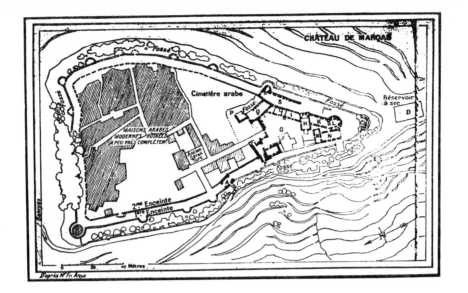

Plan of Margat
after F. Anus

fleet was lying off the coast and watching for a chance to intercept the Moslem troops. A strongly built watch-tower (Burj aṣ-Ṣabi), of the same masonry as the round keep, gave some protection to the small port, but could not hope to hold up any considerable force. The site of the castle, on the other hand, was admirable for defence, a triangular hill, rising steeply on the north and west, separated on the east by a deep valley, and only on the south joined by an easier slope to the main range. As at Krak the surrounding country was very fertile, and the castle had its economic as well as its purely defensive importance. There had been a Moslem fortress there, built, Arab authorities state, in 1062, and captured in 1117–18 by Roger of Antioch, who enfiefed it to the Mansoer family. They ceded it to the Hospitallers in the threatening year 1186. The outer wall, encircling the lower court, and strengthened with projecting semicircular towers, seems to be work of the mid-twelfth century. In the centre of the west face is a bent angle gateway (A), approached by a flight of steps over the ditch at the foot of the walls. This is a two-storeyed building, with stone brattices and a portcullis. It belongs to the same building stage as the fortifications added to the southern triangle of the castle by the Hospitallers. The latter was cut off from the lower court by a ditch, and it included a chapel (H) and a hall (F), living apartments and store rooms and the great round keep (L). The enceinte of this triangle was strengthened by a large semicircular tower on the southern point and on the eastern face by inner and outer round towers (R) superimposed upon one another. Here a deeper ditch was cut in the hillside, revetted with stone on the further side. The great hall was approached through a doorway with an elegantly moulded Gothic window, and the vaults of the roof were supported on carefully worked consols. The doorway of the chapel still has its leaf capitals, admirable examples of the refined and correct taste of the carvers employed. But the round keep is the outstanding feature of Margat. It has a diameter of 97 feet, consists of two storeys, and the roof is surrounded by a covered gallery with above it a chemin-de-ronde for manning the crenellated battlements. Made of dark basalt stone set in thick layers of mortar, it is still wonderfully complete and ranks with the greatest of the round towers of Europe, where that of Coucy, with a diameter of 106 feet, was its nearest rival till blown up by the Germans in 1918. It was not however an isolated strongpoint. A building of two storeys (K), living quarters of the knights, communicates directly with it at both levels, and, as at Krak, the defence works formed a carefully planned, concentric unit with the inner court (at Margat the southern triangle) as the final redoubt.

The castle of Margat from the south-east

In Syria the main Templar stronghold was at Tortosa, now, as already stated, a confused mass of ruins. In the plain east of the town, a region of olive groves and fertility, the Order held the small fortress of Chastel-Rouge (Yaḥmur), and some twelve miles beyond on the slopes of the hills the stronger castle of Safitha (Chastel-Blanc), from whose tower-keep, 84 feet high, Krak was visible. Placed on a conspicuous hillock between two valleys, the height of this noble, well-built tower was probably intended to provide for some form of signals. It has two storeys: the lower is a chapel whose vaults supported on pilasters are similar to those at Margat, though its incorporation into the keep results in a less decorated entrance, and a machicolation opens in the vault above the doorway; in the upper storey, a hall fills the whole extent of the tower, supported on three pillars, but lit only by arrow slits. Round the keep was an irregular enceinte with at the south-west point a large polygonal tower that must be Byzantine in inspiration, but the ground here is thickly built upon and any exact survey is impossible. On the lower slopes of the hill a polygonal wall, with only a few slight projections in it, encircled the village, with on the east a fortified gateway, but in these Templar buildings there is little of the scientific flanking that characterizes Hospitaller work. On both east and west, where approach is easiest, there seem to have been some outlying defence works. The dating of this considerable, but in its present state confused, fortress is difficult and there is little documentary help. The castle is known to have been dismantled by Nūr-ad-Dīn in 1171, at the same time as he destroyed another Templar stronghold at Arimah. In 1202 Safitha was largely overthrown by an earthquake. The keep as it stands was probably rebuilt after this destruction, but the crack visible in the apse of the chapel could date from the disaster. The remainder of the fortifications, undoubtedly rebuilt and altered, must roughly follow the original scheme.

Equalling Tortosa in scale, the Templar fortress of Château Pèlerin at Athlith is today more impressive in its ruins, and later building has not hidden its plan. It is sited on a rocky peninsula, surrounded by the sea on three sides. On the land side there is a narrow roadway, at one point passing through a rock-cut passage, rounding the slopes of Mount Carmel. Ever since in 1103 King Baldwin had been set upon and severely wounded in this defile, it had been regarded as a danger-point, and early in their career, when protection of the pilgrim routes had been their primary object, the Templars had built

CHÂTEAU PÈLERIN (ATHLITH)

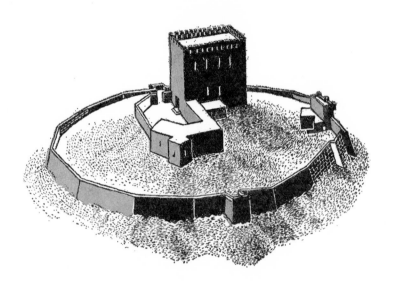

Reconstruction of the castle of Sâfithâ

an outpost here, a two storeyed tower with a small enclosure, known as Le Destroit. It was a fertile area, and the village of Athlith, an inhabited site since the Phoenician or Caananite days, had salt pans of some importance. The comparative failure of the third crusade had resulted in a treaty by which a narrow strip of coastline from Tyre to Jaffa was left in Christian hands. Acre became the new capital, and both Templars and Hospitallers had their headquarters there. The strengthening of their reduced territories became in the early thirteenth century an urgent matter for the crusaders. Little attempt was made to set up a new frontier, but the maintenance of sea communication as a source of reinforcements and also economic gain was an obvious necessity. The coming in 1217 of the fifth crusade under Andrew of Hungary and Leopold VI of Austria led to various raids into the interior, ineffectual on the whole, but enough to force a temporary Moslem withdrawal beyond Jordan. It was an opportunity for carrying out various building projects, in particular refortification of Caesarea by the Hospitallers and Austrians, and the erection of Château Pèlerin by the Templars, helped by the Teutonic knights.

South and east of the castle lay a small walled town enclosing the landing beaches of a shallow bay. It was here that Cœur-de-Lion on his march south from Acre in 1191 was supplied with food and other necessaries from the ships which *went sailing alongside the marching troops carrying their rations.* Now that the coastline was even more important, every possible landing place on this difficult coast had to be utilized. The town's defences were a single wall, of which only the foundations now exist, with a ditch and corner towers, and on the south-west point a tower on a projecting rock linked to the walls by a short causeway. Between the castle and the town was a ditch with a wall on the eastern side, and beyond it rose the imposing bulk of the main defences, a wall 13 feet thick with an inner gallery for manning casemates, a battlemented upper walk, and three gateway towers with bent angle entrances. Behind this rose another wall with two great towers, of which only the ruins of the northern still stand. Olivier the Scholastic in his *Historia Damiatina* gives a vivid account of how Phoenician coins, to him those of an unknown people, were found in the digging of the foundations. *Almost the whole time that the castle of Caesarea was being built and finished, the Templars were digging and working athwart the headland, until after working for six weeks they at last reached the bottom. There an ancient wall appeared, long and massive, and coins of a type unknown to people of today were found, provided by gift of God the Son for his knights, to lighten their expense and their toil. After that, as they were excavating and taking away sand in front, another and shorter wall was found, and, in the level space between the walls, plentiful springs of fresh water bubbled up. Plenty of stone and cement the Lord supplied also. Two towers are being erected in front of the castle, of square-hewn stones, of such a size that a single stone is hardly pulled along by two oxen to a cart. Both towers are 100 feet in length and 74 feet in width. Each contains two vaults, and their height, rising little by little, exceeds the height of the headland. Between the two towers a new and lofty wall with battlements has been completed, so wonderfully constructed that armed knights can go up and down stairs inside it.*

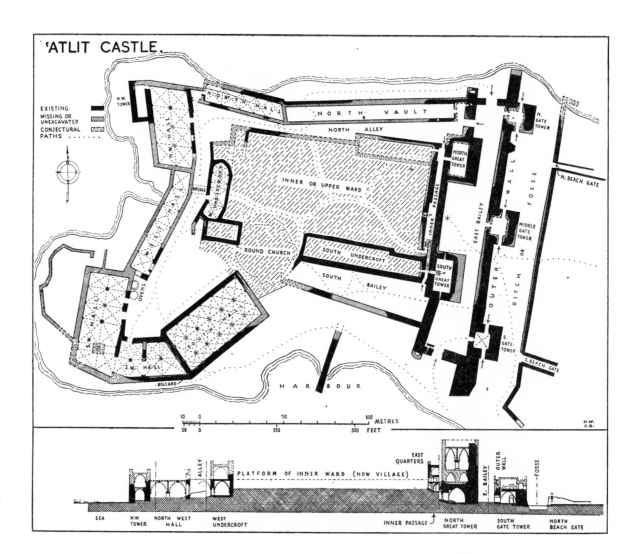

Plan of the castle of Athlith; after C. N. Johns

62

*A short distance from the towers another wall stretches from the seashore on one side across to the other, and it encloses a well of living water. From either side a new and lofty wall encircles the headland right out to the rocks. Between the south wall and the sea are two wells which give plenty of sweet water and furnish water for the castle. Within the castle there is a chapel, a hall and numerous quarters.*[16] In the northern tower the springing of the vaults can still be seen, ribs rising from carefully carved consols, two with human heads, one with smaller heads and stiff leaf foliage above them. The capital of the central column was found in the debris below. It must have been a very splendid room, but the galleries built at the western point of the promontory, with windows open to the sea, must have been even pleasanter. Within the inner ward was a dodecagonal church with three radiating chapels and vaults supported on a central pillar. Only foundations remain, but, as late as 1817, two naval officers, Irby and Mangles, could still see standing walls. *On the exterior, below the cornice, in alto-relievo, are the heads of different animals, the human with those of the lion—the ram and the sheep are particularly distinguished. The exterior walls of this edifice have a double line of arches in the Gothic style; the lower row larger than the upper one; the architecture is light and elegant.*[17] This polygonal shape recalls the Temple at Jerusalem, the Dome of the Rock, and is a native example of the round churches associated with Templar holdings in Europe. *The whole,* wrote Dr. Richard Pococke who visited Athlith in 1738, *is so magnificent, and so finely built, that it may be reckoned as one of the things that are best worth seeing in these parts.*

There was not long to wait before the defence works were severely tested. In 1220 al-ʿĀdil's son, al-Muʿaẓẓam, appeared in strength before the castle. Two years earlier he had captured and dismantled the newly restored Caesarea; and had threatened Athlith in course of construction. Now he attempted a determined siege. But the walls resisted the bombardment of his mangonels; no breach was effected, and eventually, knowing that Christian reinforcements were on the way, he withdrew. Athlith prospered. From it as a base the Templars occupied and refortified Safad and Beaufort, the former overlooking the Sea of Galilee, the latter commanding the Litany valley. Despite the severe setback of the crusading defeat at Gaza in 1244, when a combined army of Egyptians and Khorezmian Turks completely routed a Christian and Syrian Moslem force, the Templars held their ground till the arrival of Louis IX and the remnant of his force from Damietta brought some respite. In numbers it was but a LOUIS IX small reinforcement. In moral support, Louis himself meant much. New heart was put into the whole business: local feuds were reconciled: and Louis financed and encouraged the restoration of existing fortifications and the building of new, at Acre, at the constantly captured Caesarea, at Jaffa, and at Sidon. His own example was infectious. *Many a time,* wrote Joinville, *I saw the king himself carrying a hod in the trenches, to have remission of his sins.* The refortification of the seaports was Louis' main object. After the fall of Jerusalem in 1187, Saladin had left Tyre untaken, in order to press north and block the land route by which all previous crusades had come, the route in fact by which Barbarossa was to advance two years later, only to find his death in the river Saleph in Armenian Cilicia. It was by sea that the French and English armies had come, and since then it was to the sea that the crusaders looked. Jaffa, Caesarea, Acre, Sidon were the scenes of Louis' activity. *As for the great sums of money which the king expended in fortifying Jaffa, it is not expedient to speak of them, for they were beyond all reckoning, for he fortified the town from one shore to the other with twenty-four towers, and cleared the ditches from mud without and within. There were three gates, one of which the legate built, together with a curtain of wall. To give you an idea of the expense the king incurred, I may tell you that I asked the legate how much this gate and this curtain had cost him. He asked me how much I thought. And I reckoned that the gate which he had built must have cost him full two thousand five hundred crowns, and the curtain of wall one thousand five hundred. But he assured me, calling God to witness, that the gate and wall together had cost him fully fifteen thousand crowns.*[18]

63

At Acre the defences had been restored after an earthquake in 1202. Wilbrand describes it in 1212 as *a strong city* where the outer wall was commanded by the second and inner wall that overtopped it. The land round it had been at this time entrusted to the Teutonic knights, who had built or rebuilt three castles in the hills beyond the coastal plain: Mahalia, now completely lost in a more recent village; Judyn, mainly rebuilt in the eighteenth century; and Montfort, whose ruins were excavated in 1926 by the Metropolitan Museum of New York. On a typical spur site, cut by a ditch from the hillside, the first enceinte ran below the crest, the second followed closely the contours, and the keep commanded the eastern point opposite the ditch. Few of the buildings stand to any height, but some of the finds made during the excavation confirm that it was a splendid piece of architecture, with well-carved corbels, bosses and capitals, the walls painted with decorative motifs, and in the chapel grisaille glass designed with patterns and figure scenes.[19]

SIDON  While the Teutonic knights were strengthening Acre, a band of French, English, and Spanish pilgrims undertook to refortify Sidon. They had not the means to rebuild all the defences and instead, on a rocky islet, a short way from the mainland, they built a fortress with two towers and a short stone causeway, probably continued to the shore by a wooden bridge. In 1253 St. Louis, busied with an expansion of the walls of Acre, sent a party to undertake a more complete defence of Sidon, but before these reinforcements had advanced far in their work they were attacked by a force from Damascus. The sea castle held out, but the town was overrun and the townspeople massacred. The king himself now hastened north, aiding with his own hands to bury the putrefying corpses in the ruins. The castle that he built on the site of the old acropolis of Sidon still partially stands, but has been much altered by later rebuilding. Its walls formed the arc of a circle, with the keep in the centre of the arc, facing the approach to the town. There must also have been some building in the sea castle, for decorative fragments there belong to this period. At the fall of Acre some of the Templars escaped to Sidon, and it was from the sea castle that, on a dark night, they took ship for Cyprus. When al-Ashraf Khalīl entered it in July 1291, he found it empty. It remains today, now linked to the shore by a causeway, one of the most picturesque and popular of ruins.

TYRE  Between Sidon and Acre the city of Tyre required less of St. Louis' assistance. The crusading rallying point after Hattin, its defences had been put in good order. Built on a peninsula joined by a narrow isthmus, it was essentially defensible. Burchard of Mount Sion wrote of it in 1280: *It has a vast circuit of walls, greater in my opinion than that of the city of Acre, and is of a round shape, standing in the sea upon an exceeding hard rock fenced about on all sides by the sea save only on the eastern point of the city, where first Nebuchadnezzar, and afterwards Alexander, joined it to the mainland for the space of a stone's-throw. At this place it is fenced with three walls, strong and high, and twenty-five feet thick. These walls are yet further strengthened by twelve exceeding strong towers, than which I never have seen better ones in any part of the world. The citadel adjoins these towers; it is an exceeding strong castle, standing on a rock in the sea, fenced likewise with towers and strong palaces. All the world ought not to be able to take the city by fair means.*[20] But Tyre was not to stand a siege. Eleven years after Burchard wrote of it, the garrison, hearing the news of the fall of Acre, left it by night. It was destroyed by the Moslems, and never again prospered. Today it is a small village with few and inconspicuous relics of its past greatness.

TRIPOLI  Tripoli still keeps its castle, an imposing block on the landward side, but it has constantly been used as a barracks and its original plan is lost in later rebuilding. Dr. Louis Lortet visiting Tripoli in 1875, thought it: *The city of the Crusaders* par excellence. *It is still as the knights left it in 1289; nothing has been destroyed, and in walking in its picturesque thoroughfares... it seemed to me that the massive doors of these fortified houses were going to open and give passage to noble knights, clad in helmet and cuirasse, with lance and dirk in hand.*[21] But five years later when he returned he found a horse-tram, drawn by worn-out hacks, and the whole town in course of a shabby modernization.

Beirut had a very different history. Captured by Saladin in 1187, it was retaken for the Christians in 1197 by a German force under Henry of Lorraine working in co-operation with the Cypriot fleet. Aimery of Cyprus gave the town to his brother-in-law, John of Ibelin, the Old Lord of Beirut, who was to lead the opposition to Frederick II. Under his rule (c. 1198–1236), Beirut knew a period of prosperity. Wilbrand of Oldenburg in 1212 thus describes the castle: *On the lowest part it is fortified by the sea and precipitous rocks, and on the other by a ditch with walls, deep enough so that we could see in it several captives confined as in a prison. Two strong walls overlook this ditch, in which towers have been very powerfully erected against the attack of machines, and the stones of which are linked by great iron bars. In one of these towers, recently rebuilt, we saw a most ornate palace, which I will briefly describe. It is well planned and sited, looking out on one side on the sea and the ships leaving the harbour, on the other on meadows, orchard, and very pleasant places. The pavement is made of mosaic, simulating water lightly moved by wind, so that he who advances on it seems to walk; but leaves no footprint on its painted sand. The walls are covered with marble, the roof is painted with fleeting clouds, zephyr blowing and the sun dividing the years and months, the days and weeks, the hours and minutes by his movement in the zodiac. In all of which, Syrians, Saracens and Greeks have vied with most delectable competition in the mastery of their arts. In the midst of the palace is a well, constructed with very varied marbles, formed into patterns of flowers, with in the centre a gaping dragon pursuing other beasts there depicted, and from it a fountain rises into the air, moistening and cooling it, and lulling to sleep with its soft murmur.*[22]

Beirut capitulated to Khalīl after the fall of Acre, and was one of the few ports not dismantled. It early regained some commercial importance and was from 1585 to 1635 the capital of the almost independent and splendid rule of Fakhr-ad-Dīn. William Bartlett's drawing of 1834 shows the great castle, with its high central keep still standing, with a smaller fortress, reached by a bridge, controlling the harbour. These fortifications suffered severely in the English bombardment of 1840, when the Western powers drove out Ibrāhīm Pasha. In 1875 Lortet shows the ruins of the castle as still visible, but with the rapid growth of the city all this area was rebuilt, and even the site of John of Ibelin's palace cannot now be traced.

Further north the port of Latakia was captured by Saladin in 1188 and largely destroyed. *It was,* writes ʿImād ad-Dīn, *a rich city, palaces everywhere and marble porticoes. Our emirs took these fine marbles and had them transported to their houses in Syria.* Retaken in 1200, the fortifications must have been repaired, but the castle on the rising ground south-east of the town was destroyed when Kalavun captured the town in 1287. Until a severe earthquake in 1822 the port castle seems to have remained standing; *a fine old castle projecting into the sea,* Irby and Mangles call it in 1818, but by 1824 John Madox describes the harbour as blocked by its fallen ruins.[23] Today something of it can still be seen, bonded insecurely with ancient columns.

In the feverish building activities of the first half of the thirteenth century two Templar undertakings, additional to the builders of Athlith, were the refortification of Safad and Beaufort (Shaqīf Ar- nūn). Safad controlled the western shore of the Sea of Galilee and the route westwards from it, the main route from Damascus. A castle had been built there by Fulk of Anjou between 1138 and 1140, probably one of his quadrilaterals with corner towers. It successfully defied Saladin after his victory at nearby Hattin, but surrendered to his brother al-ʿĀdil in 1188 after the fall of Jerusalem. In 1220 in their temporary retreat beyond Jordan the Moslems had dismantled it. The negotiations conducted in 1240 by Theobald IV of Champagne, with the threat of further reinforcements under Richard of Cornwall behind him, obtained its return to Christian hands. The account of its construction is given in an anonymous contemporary chronicle, probably by Benedict of Alignan, who plays the main part in it. He was bishop of Marseilles and in 1239 or 1240 had visited Damascus during a truce. There he was constantly asked whether the Christians were going to rebuild Safad, *the key to the gate of Damascus*. The bishop on his return went to the Grand Master, Armand de Périgord, who was sick at Acre, and urged him to undertake the rebuilding. The Master explained to him that the king of Navarre and the duke of Burgundy had just given up the attempt, and how could the Templars without a subsidy undertake it. *Then the Bishop said 'Master, rest in your bed, and send your good will and words of authority to the brothers, and I trust in God that you will do more from your bed than the whole army has done with its multitude of armed men and abundance of riches'.*[24] The bishop addressed the Council of the Templars saying that though he had no money for the work he would preach to the pilgrims and lead them out from Acre to build the castle. Under his inspiring leadership a party set out from Acre, and the work was successfully carried through. Twenty years later, in July 1266, Safad fell to Baybars; its Templar garrison were executed, and their skulls piled up as a trophy.

Whatever the exact history of its building, the castle must have been on an impressive scale. On a steep hill-top, its outer enceinte was roughly elliptical in form, separated by a ditch from the inner defences. Rey, visiting it in 1863, found on the raised ground of the inner court the remains of a rectangular keep. Guérin in 1875 describes, in some detail, the foundations of a circular keep, 34 metres in diameter, rising from a talus. This, if the measurements are correct, would have been larger than the round tower of Margat. Today it is impossible to decide between these discrepant accounts. Safad suffered severe destruction, with much loss of life, in an earthquake in 1837. The town was largely rebuilt with stones taken from the castle which had become, Guérin noted, *A veritable quarry, from which the inhabitants of the town continually extracted materials, already worked, to build new houses.* The crusading citadel disappeared under these deprivations and is partially covered by the modern thriving township.[25]

BEAUFORT Built on the crest of a cliff face rising steeply above the bend in the Litany valley where the river turns westward to reach the sea north of Tyre, Beaufort has from below the most dramatic silhouette of all crusading castles. To the north-west the ground slopes more gradually towards the foothills above Sidon, and this was the only practical approach to the castle. The site was strong for defence, ill-placed for rapid attack. But in this raiding warfare between Damascus and the coast, it held a central position where a garrison could await some favourable opportunity. Saladin kept a siege force before it for a year until it surrendered, starved out, in 1190. The castle had originally been built by Fulk of Anjou, about 1140, and the square keep, surrounded by an irregular polygonal enclosure, following the contours of the crest, probably dates from this period. It was held by the lords of Sidon, and it was Reginald of Sidon who held it at the time of the defeat of Hattin. Either shortly before or immediately after this battle the defence works were extended to form a complex bent entrance and ramp. Some of this work was according to Arab chroniclers carried out while Reginald was negotiating its surrender with Saladin. This remarkable man was an example of the orientalized Frank. Versed in Arabic, which he both spoke and read, appreciative of Arab learning and culture, he had acquired also something of their diplomatic subtlety. Saladin found him a congenial companion. But it became clear that there was trickery at work. Reginald, playing his dangerous game to the last, found himself in Moslem hands and faced with the demand that the castle should surrender. Taken to the walls, Reginald instead exhorted the garrison not to give way, and when tied by the arms to a tree continued to urge resistance, while his men shot at him to try and end his agony. Saladin sent him as a prisoner to Banyas, but eventually agreed to his release as part of the terms of surrender. They were to meet again when Reginald in 1191 was entrusted with an embassy, and Saladin welcomed him as a distinguished guest.

66

*A tent was prepared for him,* wrote Bahā'-ad-Dīn, *full of cushions and carpets worthy of a king.* It is one of the strangest and at the same time most revealing episodes of crusading history.

Al-ʿĀdil Abū-Bakr, after the death of Saladin, undertook a restoration and expansion of many of the castles that had passed into his hands. He was a great builder, and his masons employed a particular type of boss on their ashlar that is recognizable on some of the outer enceinte of Beaufort, particularly on a tower rising from a great round glacis at the south-west corner, now the most striking and best preserved part of the ruins. In 1240 Beaufort was handed over with Safad to the Templars, who must have built the Gothic hall in the central courtyard, much ruined since Rey drew its elegant doorway. In 1268 the castle was taken by Baybars, who allowed the women and children to depart to Tyre, but slaughtered the combatants.

TORON (TIBNIN)

The castle of Toron (Tibnin) had a somewhat similar history. Built originally by Hugh of St. Omer in 1102 to cut off the Moslem garrison in Tyre from Damascus, it became an important crusading stronghold, frequently mentioned by the chroniclers. Captured by Saladin in 1187, it was restored to the crusaders in 1229 by the treaty between Frederick II and al-Kāmil. Given by the Emperor to the heiress of the lords of Toron, who later married Philip of Montfort, it was refortified, but fell to Baybars in 1266. Today Toron has standing walls with semicircular towers, impressive enough, but they date from its rebuilding by Daher-al-ʿUmar, who for a time occupied Sidon and the surrounding country in the later eighteenth century.

CHÂTEAU NEUF (ḤŪNĪN) L'ASSEBEIBE (AṢ-ṢUBAIBA)

East of Toron, on either side of the valley running from Damascus to Lake Hulah, were the castles of Château Neuf (Ḥūnīn) and L'Assebeibe (Qalʿat aṣ-Ṣubaiba). The former still has the foundations of its rectangular enceinte, and its rock-cut ditches, but otherwise little remains. Aṣ-Ṣubaiba is a more extensive ruin, on a steep hillside above the town of Banyas. It was built between the years 1129 and 1132, after Banyas had been ceded to the crusaders by the Ismailian sect in return for territory in the Anṣārīyah mountains. It was, however, only held by the Franks for three years. It was retaken by them in 1140, in alliance with Damascus against ʿImād-ad-Dīn Zengi of Mosul. Hard pressed by Nūr-ad-Dīn in 1157, it was only the determined resistance of the constable, Humphrey of Toron, that forced his withdrawal even when the outer wall had been battered to the ground in many places. Baldwin III hastened to repair the castle and the town walls, summoning masons from all the neighbouring cities. It was only at the third attempt, in 1164, that Nūr-ad-Dīn succeeded in taking Ṣubaiba, while the main forces of the Kingdom were campaigning in Egypt. Despite various attempts, it was never regained. The Sire de Joinville gives a vivid account of the last crusading attack in 1253, and tells how the castle is *fully half a league up the mountains of Libanu, and the acclivity which goes up to it is scattered all over with rocks as big as meal tubs.* The Marquis de Vogüé, writing in 1876, echoes Joinville's memories of the rough ascent: *This morning, before leaving Banias, we have made the ascent to the castle which dominates the village and which the Arabs call Kalat-es-Sebaibah. Built, ruined, rebuilt, extended turn by turn by Templars and Saracens, the citadel of Banias is perhaps one of the strongest, the best preserved and the most interesting of all those with which the Crusades have crowned the mountains of Palestine. An hour and a half was needed to climb with hands and feet the rough path that leads to this abandoned eagle's nest. More than once we hesitate at the labour, and take to blushing at our feebleness in thinking that the Crusaders, men of French tongue and Christian hearts, have taken these escarpments by repeated assaults. I have re-read yesterday evening the account in Joinville of the expedition which Saint Louis sent to Tyre. The sight of these places lends a singular eloquence and perfect clarity to the old seneschal's narration. Happier than the men of arms of the Count of Eu, we gain without impediment the walls of the castle, where the jackals alone keep garrison, and we penetrate the enceinte by the postern in one of the towers. The water still stagnates in the vast abandoned cisterns which once supplied*

The castle of Montréal (ash-Shaubak)

*the place; the fig trees and the wall-plants cling to the broken stairways, climb on the platforms of the towers and peer curiously through the crenellations.*[26]

The outer walls follow the indentations of the hillside and stretch along it for a length of 1400 feet. The keep is on the highest point of the ground, a rectangular two-storeyed building, surrounded by an outer wall. Today it is a confused mass of ruins, from which no clear details emerge. Westward from it stretched the lower court, with on the western face, where the approach is more gradual, four large rectangular towers which seem to be mainly Arab work. The round towers of the south face and south-east corner are also Arab work, clearly marked by their particular method of cutting bosses on the face of the stones. There are several Arab inscriptions throughout the building.

MONTRÉAL (ASH-SHAUBAK) Another castle where Arab workmanship remains the conspicuous and most splendid feature is that of Kerak or Petra deserti, the chief crusading castle of 'la terre oultre le Jourdain'. As early as 1100 the crusaders had journeyed as far south as Petra, but in 1115 Baldwin I began a more permanent occupation by founding the castle of Montréal (ash-Shaubak), which still, though mainly later rebuilding, crowns its hilltop, with a long spiral stairway of 365 steps, cut by the crusaders, leading down to a subterranean spring. *There, in an elevated spot well suited to his purpose, he built a fortress strongly defended by its natural site and by artificial means. When the work was finished, he placed a garrison of both cavalry and infantry forces there and granted them extensive possessions. The place was fortified with walls, towers, forewalls, and a moat, and was well equipped with arms, and machines. Since a king was its founder, he gave it a*

The castle of Kerak (Petra deserti) from the south

*name derived from the royal prestige and called it Montréal. The spot has the advantage of fertile soil, which produces abundant supplies of grain, wine, and oil. Moreover, it is especially noted for its healthful and delightful location. This fortress dominated the entire district adjacent to it.*[27]

The following year Baldwin led another expedition down to al-ʿAqabah on the Red Sea, fortifying the town and the neighbouring island of Graye. In the course of these journeys the crusaders had occupied and probably fortified the town of Kerak to the east of the Dead Sea on the pilgrim route from Damascus to the Red Sea and Mecca, but it was not till 1142 that Payen le Bouteiller began the castle there. It was an ancient site with some old buildings that could be used to supplement the local stone, a reddish-black volcanic tufa, difficult to work. The crusading buildings here are in fact of rude craftsmanship; the masonry is roughly squared, and the walls, with rectangular projecting towers, have little scientific planning in their alignment, though their ditches and in places paved glacis strengthen their defences. A wide ditch across the spur of the hill separated the castle from the town, which formed a kind of lower court. On the opposite south face another ditch and a long open cistern cut off the castle from the main hillside. But Kerak, if its strength was less fair than that of the northern fortresses, was a redoubtable strong point. It was to the Moslems *the wolf which fate has brought into this valley and the excuse for those who abandon the duty of pilgrimage prescribed by God. Kerak and Shaubak recall this verse of the poet speaking of two lions: Not a day passes, but they devour human flesh and drink blood.* In 1174 the lady of Kerak, Etienne of Milly, took as her third husband Reginald of Châtillon, at one

69

time Prince of Antioch, but driven from the principality by his freebooting ways. From Kerak he began to raid pilgrim caravans, and even launched pirate ships in the Red Sea, activities which finally provoked Saladin first to two determined but unsuccessful sieges of Kerak and then in 1187 to the decisive campaign against the Kingdom and the battle of Hattin, where the largest force that the crusaders could muster was completely routed. Reginald, taken prisoner in the battle, was executed. For him there could be no clemency, but to his widow, when she appealed for the release of her son, Humphrey of Toron, by her first marriage, Saladin offered the young man's liberty in return for the surrender of Kerak. Mother and son travelled south to Kerak to carry out the transaction, but the defenders refused to accept the agreement. Humphrey, honouring his mother's pledge, returned to captivity. In 1188 a force under Saladin's son-in-law invested Kerak. The garrison, without any recognized leader, for the baronage was scattered or dead, held out for five months, even though half starved, before they surrendered. Montréal was blockaded for a year and a half before it fell, and it was said that, cut off from any salt, many of the garrison became blind.

Kerak was given by Saladin to his brother and eventual successor, al-ʿĀdil Abū-Bakr. Here he built on the south front the great keep, rising from the rock face with its side walls at obtuse angles to the front, composed of stone imported from a quarry at some distance and more easily cut than the local volcanic rock. It has the bosses that characterize al-ʿĀdil's work. Kerak was never again to be in Christian hands. When in 1219 al-Kāmil offered to restore Jerusalem and Galilee to the crusaders if they raised the siege of Damietta, the latter replied that they must have Kerak also, and negotiations were abandoned. Ten years later, in the treaty with Frederick II, the castles of 'La Terre oultre le Jourdain' were expressly excluded. The great crusading revival of the thirteenth century left them untouched.

Of Arab castles in Syria in the earlier part of the twelfth century there is little certain evidence. It is not till Nūr-ad-Dīn that a new impetus becomes apparent. It is known that he worked on the citadel at Aleppo, that wonderful silhouette on its great ancient tell, but here the enceinte is mainly later rebuilding: the towers of the triple gateways are the work of aẓ-Ẓāhir Ghāzi, Saladin's profuse and ambitious son, as was also the facing of the tell with smooth slabs, a characteristic embellishment of the defences used also at the Antiochene fortress of Harim after its recapture by the Arabs, and still visible on the mound at Homs where once stood the citadel.

SALADIN'S WORK AT CAIRO   Saladin's own fortifications can be most clearly seen in the northern enclosure of the citadel of Cairo; a curtain reinforced by semicircular towers of moderate projection, generally in direct contact with the platform walk and furnished with three loopholes, widely splayed slits spanned by a lintel, and an almost flat relieving arch. In the citadel and in the Burj aẓ-Ẓafar, at the north-east corner of the city wall, are bent entrances, the first certainly known in Arab fortification since the round city at Baghdad. Saladin began to build in 1176 and most of his work was presumably completed when he left Cairo for the last time in 1182. The small fortress built by his orders in 1185 in the Wadi Sadr opposite Suez has round towers at the gateway and the main angle of the defences.

AL-ʿĀDIL'S BUILDINGS:   But it is with al-ʿĀdil that we reach the great period of Moslem castle building. The Western power was reviving; Cœur-de-Lion's campaigns had shown what a genuine menace still lay in the Franks. The large scale and splendid masonry of al-ʿĀdil's buildings are a major act of policy in the attempt to hold together his brother's conquests, and an example which the contemporary Arab rulers followed, even perhaps borrowing masons from his yard. At the central point of his territory, the citadel of DAMASCUS   Damascus, built around and enclosed as it is today, is still his greatest monument. Standing on flat ground, protected on one side by the twin streams of the Banyas canal and the river Barada, it relied on its own strength to hold its key position at the exposed corner of the town defences. Covering an

The castle of ʿAjlūn

area 500 feet from north to south and 750 feet from east to west, with thirteen large rectangular towers occupying more than half the perimeter, it represents a complete replanning of the older stronghold that had been partially rebuilt by Saladin. Here we find the main features of the style of al-ʿĀdil's masons. Large rusticated blocks, rectangular towers of great size, strongly vaulted interior compartments, arrow slits roofed with a tapering vault, and considerable use of stone brattices. At Cairo too, though less sweepingly, al-ʿĀdil strengthened Saladin's work, adding additional rectangular towers (the Burj at-Tuffar is 96 feet square) and encasing six of Saladin's round towers in towers of much greater size (Burj ar-Ramla and Burj al-Haddād), though here retaining their circular form. Elsewhere al-ʿĀdil, or his immediate dependents, were responsible for the Moslem fortress on Mt. Tabor, for much of the fortification at Baalbek, bringing the temple of Bacchus and the temple of Jupiter into one system and converting the former into a keep, and at Bosrah for the ingenious conversion of the Roman theatre into a powerful castle. Throughout the captured Frankish castles his additions and restorations are frequently evident.

A small but exactly dated and reasonably preserved Arab castle may be taken as a summary of these developments: ʿAjlūn built in 1184–5 by ʿIzz ad-dīn Usāmah, one of Saladin's emirs, on a hilltop opposite Belvoir, overlooking the Jordan valley.[28] The castle was a quadrilateral, with four square corner towers, and baileys on the southern and eastern sides. The hillside was cut into a rock ditch in which a pillar for a bridge was left standing. Some thirty years later the castle was enlarged by Aibak

ʿAJLŪN

71

Ibn-ʿAbdullāh, one of the most active builders among al-ʿĀdil's followers. He added a large rectangular tower, typical of his master's general designs, to the south bailey, in accordance with the general trend towards enlarging the outer defences. The building of both periods is in rusticated masonry. A conspicuous landmark, ʿAjlūn is a ready reminder that the crusaders held no monopoly of the art of fortification. They had in fact learned much from the Arabs. The bent entrance and the use of brattices above the doorways or continuous machicolation along the walls were features for which eastern prototypes are numerous. The facing of slopes with a paved stone glacis was practised by the crusaders before it became familiar in the West. The pointed arch that early appears in crusading churches, the godrons that decorate the porch of the Holy Sepulchre had alike Eastern inspiration. No Arab castle of the time equals Krak des Chevaliers in planning or in execution, but by then the Franks had proved themselves apt pupils.

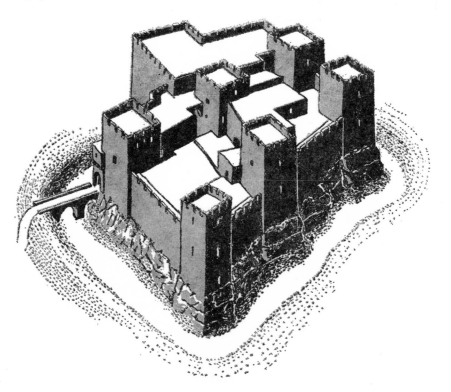

Reconstruction of
the castle of ʿAjlūn.

SHAIZAR

Two Arab castles, neither of which can boast the work of al-ʿĀdil's masons, deserve some notice, for their associations rather than their remains. To the north-west of Hamah on a rock enclosed on two sides by the Orontes is the castle of Shaizar, now, except for the buildings on its northern and southern extremities, a confused and fairly ruinous village. Often attacked by the crusaders, it was never held by them, and in the first half of the twelfth century belonged to the Munqidh family. It was here that Usāmah ibn-Munqidh, whose autobiography is the most personal document of crusading history, was brought up and made his first contacts with the Franks. Critical of their ignorance on many matters but admiring of their courage, he writes of the strange, chivalrous but fierce communications between them. Visits were exchanged in moments of truce. *A few months later there came to us a letter from Tancred, the lord of Antioch, carried by a knight accompanied with attendants and followers. The letter read: 'This is a revered knight of the Franks who has completed the holy pilgrimage and is now on his way back to his country. He has asked me to introduce him to you so that he may see your cavaliers. Accordingly, I have sent him to you.*

The castle of Shaizar

*Treat him well.' The knight was a young man, handsome in looks and well dressed; but his body bore traces of numerous cuts. His face showed the mark of a sword blow which had cut him from the middle of his head to the fore part of his face. I asked about him and was told: 'This is the one who made a charge against the army of the Isbaslar Mawdud, whose horse was killed and who fought until he rejoined his comrades.' Exalted is Allah who can do what he pleases as he pleases! Holding aloof no more retards fate than adventure hastens it.*[29]

Then in 1157 the whole of this district was devastated by a particularly severe earthquake and the fortress seems to have been almost entirely destroyed. Nūr-ad-Dīn restored it, but the main works as they stand today are probably from the first half of the thirteenth century. The square keep of fine masonry, with a rock-cut ditch beyond it, controls the northern, least naturally defended side. On the south a stone bridge has replaced the medieval drawbridge, and the entry lies through a gate tower. Beyond this the rock has been faced with a great glacis, above which are the ruins of a large tower. This last must have been a work of imposing strength, planned with care and considerable skill, but the walls that linked it with the keep seem to have had little thickness and little projection in their rectangular towers.

FAMIA
(QAL'AT AL-MUDĪQ)
North of Shaizar overlooking the Orontes valley can still be traced the walls and streets of the important Seleucid town of Apamea. A small hill, partially artificial, marks the ancient citadel and is

Famia (Qal'at al-Mudīq)

now the village of Qal'at al-Muḍiq. Occupied by Tancred in 1106 and known as Famia, it was captured by Nūr-ad-Dīn in 1139 and from then on was in Moslem hands. There seems never to have been a keep or central strongpoint. The walls follow the oval of the hilltop with a gateway between two towers and rectangular towers, some of them of fine masonry, at regular intervals. Famia suffered from the great earthquake of 1157, and, to judge by surviving inscriptions, its existing defences date from the thirteenth century.

THE ASSASSINS

In the deeply enclosed valleys of the Ansārīyah mountains, a fertile but not easily accessible district, a people known as the Ismailians had settled about 1120, with the connivance if not actually in alliance with the crusaders. They were a Shiite sect, opposed alike to the Sunnite Caliphate of Baghdad and to the Selchükids. At the end of the eleventh century their leader, Ḥasan-i-Ṣabbāh, had organized them into a fanatical band, pledged to unswerving obedience to himself, and subdued to his will by a controlled distribution of the drug hashish. Political murder became his chief weapon, and his followers, trained to suicidal devotion, became adept practitioners; from their drug they received the name Assassins, and their deeds gave to it the most sinister implications. From a remote stronghold in the Alamut valley of Khurasan, where fragments of his castle still cling to a fantastically shaped rock, ALAMUT Ḥasan in 1092 organized the murder of Niẓām al-Mulk, the great reforming vizier of Baghdad, who would have driven these dangerous neighbours from their stronghold but could not penetrate the mountains that protect it. Ridvan of Aleppo, a ruler of uncertain orthodoxy, brought a detachment of them into Syria, but on his death in 1113 they were driven out of Aleppo. In 1126 they are found, momentarily protected by Damascus, at Banyas, and when the Damascene ruler changed, they came to terms with the Franks, handed over Banyas to them, and occupied in exchange some territory in the Ansārīyah mountains. There they existed for a time, comparatively unnoticed, except for the murder in 1152 of Raymond II of Tripoli, the motives for which were never solved and may well have lain in the intricacies of Raymond's private life. In 1169 a new leader came from Alamut, Rāshid ad-Dīn Sinān, who was to be known to the crusaders as 'The Old Man of the Mountains'. His headquarters was at Maṣyāf, where his castle, now a patchwork of different dates, still stands with its walls complete, MAṢYĀF though constant rebuilding has obscured its original defensive plan, never probably a very clear one. Masyaf lies due west of Hamah where the road turns north to the Orontes valley, and various tracks lead into the Ansārīyah mountains, eventually reaching the sea coast. It was a key position, and was in particular of importance to Saladin in his northern campaign of 1188. Though he himself marched up the coast road to Latakia, he could not, with Tortosa and Margat in Christian hands, use it as a supply route. His campaign against Antioch had to be supplied from his base at Hamah by inland routes, which passed close to Assassin strongholds. As the destroyer of the Fatimite and Shiite Caliphate of Cairo, he was peculiarly obnoxious to the Ismailians, and in 1176 he had actually laid siege to Maṣyāf. What happened there is only known to us in detail from an account written in praise of Sinān, but it seems that an emissary, despite all precautions, penetrated to Saladin's tent, leaving a knife by his pillow. There is no doubt that the Assassins had an unnerving quality; Saladin made his peace with them, and in 1188 was able to use the route through their territory. Conrad of Montferrat, the defender of Tyre, was killed by an Assassin in 1191, very shortly after his recognition as king of Jerusalem. The crusaders seem from then on to have had more to fear from this source than had the Moslems. When Wilbrand of Oldenburg visited the coastal towns in 1212, he wrote of Tortosa that it was *on the boundaries of the Old Man of the Mountain* (antiquus de montanis), *who is wont through his messengers to kill our men with daggers;* and of Margat that *opposed to it there are many strong castles of the Old Man of the Mountain.*

Some of these 'strong castles', in addition to Maṣyāf, still exist in states of varying ruin, merging with the rocks on which they stand. Qalʿat Aleika, al-Qadmūs, one of the Ismailians' earliest possessions, and al-Kahf, approached only by a tunnel in the rock and the last of the Assassin strongholds to fall to Baybars in 1273, are in the hills to the west of Maṣyāf. Qalʿat Abū-Qubais lay to the north, between Masyaf and Shaizar. Beni Israel was the northernmost of the Assassin castles, controlling a rough hill track that ran from the Orontes valley to the port of Jabala. It was surrendered to Saladin, probably as a result of negotiations on his northern campaign. Some walls of squared masonry still stand, but no clear plan can be established, and it was almost certainly a walled enclosure with some slight projections, similar to Maṣyāf. Roughly built, generally on earlier foundations, these Assassin strongholds have little architectural interest, but the remote valleys which they dominate are luxuriant and unvisited, and legends easily linger there.

The Assassins make a final and remarkable appearance in crusading history, when, on the arrival of Louis IX at Acre, they sent a threatening message to him, demanding release from the tribute paid by them to the Templars and Hospitallers. Joinville thus describes the interview: *The king made them sit down, and in front of the others was an emir, well dressed and handsomely armed; and behind him sat a bachelor, also well appointed, who held in his hand three knives, the blade of one fitted into the handle of another, because, if the emir had been refused, he would have presented these three knives to the king in token of defiance. Behind him who held the three knives sat another with a shroud twisted round his arm, which likewise he would have presented to the king to bury him in, had he refused the demand of the Old Man of the Mountain.* St. Louis was not the man to be frightened by such dumb shows. Next day he interviewed the messenger again, this time seated between the Grand Masters of the two Orders. They soon called the embassy to order, and *within a fortnight* it was back, this time with gifts. *Among other curiosities which he sent to the king was a crystal elephant, very well carved, and an animal they call a giraffe, also in crystal, balls of divers sorts in crystal, and backgammon and chessboards, and all these were ornamented with amber, and the amber was attached to the crystal by fair filigree of pure gold. As soon as the envoys opened the coffers in which these things were packed, it seemed as if the whole chamber were filled with spices, so fragrantly did they smell.* The king in his turn sent gifts back to the Old Man, and accompanying them Brother Yves the Breton, who spoke Arabic and who on his return had much to tell of what he had seen. *When the Old Man rode out on horse-back, there went a crier before him, bearing a Danish battle-axe, with a long haft all covered with silver, and stuck all over with knives, and he cried aloud, 'Turn aside from before him who carries the death of kings in his hands.'* [30] But as yet the crusading strongholds, Krak, Sāfithā and Margat were strong enough to keep these fanatics in check.

One more opportunity remained for the crusaders. In 1258 the Mongols under Hulagu, whose Nestorian wife influenced him towards a pro-Christian policy, captured Baghdad and overthrew the Caliphate. In 1260, accompanied by Hetoum of Armenia and Bohemond of Antioch, Hulagu entered Damascus. Here was a new hope for Christendom, but the barons at Acre hesitated. When a Mamluk army marched north from Egypt, they gave it free passage, and no Frankish force joined with Hulagu's son, Kitbogha, when he met and was defeated by the Egyptians at ʿAin Jālūt in 1260, a battle that was decisive for Mamluk and Moslem supremacy on the eastern coastline of the Mediterranean. There were to be no more postponements.

In 1265 Baybars marched from Egypt through crusading territory. The town of Athlith was sacked in 1265, though he did not assault the castle. *It stands in the deep sea,* wrote Burchard of it in 1280, *and is fenced with walls and outworks, and such strong barbicans and towers that the whole world ought not to be able to take it.* It was in fact never taken. After the loss of Acre, the knights evacuated it and withdrew to Cyprus. Mamluk forces entered and partly dismantled it, but it never was garrisoned. In the early

The Assassin castle of Maṣyāf

nineteenth century much of it was still standing. Lamartine in 1833, not knowing even its name, could exercise his poetic talent on these evocative ruins: *We had since morning on the horizon before us, on the seashore, an immense column which reflected the rays of the sun and which seemed to grow in size and to emerge from the waves as we advanced. Drawing nearer, we recognize that this column is a confused mass of magnificent ruins belonging to different epochs; we distinguish first an immense wall, resembling by its form, its colour, and the squaring of its stones, a section of the Colosseum at Rome. This wall, of a prodigious height, stands, alone and detached, on a heap of other ruins of Greek and Roman construction; soon we discover, beyond the stretch of wall, remains of a monument in the moresque style, traceried like lacework in stone, a church or a mosque, or perhaps both in turn; then a series of other ruins, of antique construction, standing and well preserved; the sand track which our guides followed led us close enough to this curious debris of the past, of whose existence we had been completely ignorant, knowing neither its name nor date.*[31] Then in 1837 Ibrāhīm Pasha blew up the ruins to secure building material to repair the walls of Acre. Athlith became a quarry, and a small, poverty-stricken village inhabited its ruins, until in 1930 the Department of Antiquities in Palestine began their never completed excavation of the site.

Three years after the loss of Athlith, Jaffa fell. Walls, citadel, and churches were razed to the ground, JAFFA FALLS and Baybars sent the marble from them to decorate the mosque that he was building in Cairo. One by one the last Frankish strongholds were falling. Renewed schemes for a Mongol alliance, the coming of Edward of England, these were but flickers of encouragement, inadequate to change the oncoming

77

events. In 1268 Antioch, still a wealthy city, was stormed by Baybars, and a terrible massacre followed. The great circuit of walls was still intact, but there had been insufficient men to guard them.

Antioch in the thirteenth century had played little part in general crusading policy. Its rulers had been undistinguished, dissolute men, largely dominated by the more vigorous rulers of Armenia, to

whom they were bound by marriage alliances. The port of Latakia was the point at which the principality had closest touch with crusading policies, and Latakia survived as a Christian port for nineteen years after the loss of the northern capital. Communication between the two had however never been easy. The thickly wooded slopes of Mt. Silpius and Mt. Cassius (to the Franks Mons Parlerius) blocked the passage to the north, and only rough tracks led through it. Only one castle of any note is to be

found in this unfrequented area, that of Cursat (Quṣair), owned by the Latin patriarchs of Antioch. It was refortified in 1256 and the two large horseshoe towers that still stand must date from this period, for they are built on to earlier work. In shape they are similar to the towers of Armenian castles, but their masonry is finer than normal Armenian work and achieves the high Frankish standard.

The coastal route from Latakia to St. Simeon made an inland detour round Mt. Cassius, and this seems to have been frequently used in the twelfth century. Alternatively two routes led eastward to

the Orontes valley, both over mountainous country. The northern, now the main road, was only watched by the castle of Aidho, whose vague ruins are undocumented; the southern by Haffe, with Saone lying to the south, went through steep hilly country. Both routes lead to the bridge over the Orontes at Jisr ash-Shogr, where the roads from Aleppo to Latakia and from Hamah to Antioch cross the river. Round this crossways there were a group of castles. South of the bridge overlooking the track running on the west side of the Orontes were the castles of Sarminyah and Bourzey. North was

the important stronghold of Bakas-Shogr. All these castles were taken by Saladin in his northern campaign, a necessary step to ensure his lines of communication, and none was again in Christian hands. After the capture of Saone Saladin had occupied Balathanos (Qalaʿat Mahalbe), whose walls still show a mixture of Byzantine and Frankish masonry, thereby opening up a mountainous route via Beni-Israel to the Orontes valley. Then, taking the northern road from Latakia to Jisr ash-Shogr, he proceeded to lay siege to Bakas-Shogr. The castle lies on a spur of mountain, which runs roughly north and south, projecting into the stream Nahr al-Abiad and causing a horseshoe bend in it. The spur slopes downwards from the mountain ending in a cliff-face above the river; in its centre it sinks to a narrow ridge, so that it is in fact composed of two rocks, with a natural barrier between them. The weakest point was, as always, where the spur joins the hillside. Here a considerable ditch was cut, and the strongest fortifications to judge from existing remains were concentrated on its northern side: the general scheme is reminiscent of Saone, though never carried out with the same elaboration. Saladin was able to bring his mangonels up the hillside and force an entry into the upper castle; the besieged then retreated into the lower castle, destroying the drawbridge across the middle ditch. Saladin could not, at least without much delay, bring his mangonels across the upper ditch or up the cliff-sides of the spur. The lower castle remained out of reach of their projection, and it seemed as though the garrison might have to be starved out. There was, however, little hope of the feeble and dissolute Bohemund III of Antioch coming to their rescue, and the morale of the Principality was notably inferior to that of the coast towns. After a three days' truce, the garrison surrendered.

Saladin then turned to the reduction of the castles of Sarminyah and Bourzey. The former, of no great size, was easily stormed and seems to have been very thoroughly destroyed. Bourzey was a very different matter. General Sir John Hackett, in a thesis written some thirty years ago, has given a vivid description of the site and a reconstruction of the course of the siege. *Like so many other castles in Syria, Bourzey is built on a mountain spur, projecting in an easterly direction from the high ground of the Ansariyah*

The castle of Yilan. See page 81

*range, and falling abruptly on three sides to the level of the Orontes Valley. On its north and south sides steep, rough wadis filled with great boulders and scrub, and very hard going, lead up to the high ground to the west of the castle where the village now stands. The level here is about 100 feet lower than the base of the walls. On the day after his arrival (20th August) Saladin rode his horse round the castle to find a place to attack it. The west seemed to be the only possible direction from which he could approach, and he had a tent erected for himself there and took up a position with light-armed troops. Ibn al-Athīr says there was no room for any others. He managed to get up a mangonel and bring it to bear on the western wall of the castle, but it was on lower ground, and one well-aimed mangonel from the castle neutralized its fire. Saladin despaired of achieving anything by bombardment and devised a plan to utilize his superior numbers, and turn the length of the castle's walls to his advantage. He divided his army into three divisions to deliver successive assaults, hoping, while maintaining the strength of his own soldiers by periods of rest, to wear the garrison down by continuous exertion. On the morning of the 23rd the first division delivered its attack under 'Imad-ad-Din Zengi, prince of Sinjar. The garrison left the citadel and manned the outer rampart, delivering a heavy volume of fire from their bowmen and rolling down great stones. The Saracens protected themselves with 'cats' and similar shelters and from behind them did a certain amount of damage with their arrows. But as they approached the western wall the slope, as it steepened, began to slow them up and the stones and arrows of the Franks grew more effective. When it could get no further the first division was withdrawn (their teeth on edge with the length of the fight), and the second sent in. This consisted of the Sultan's own household troops, and Saladin himself and his nephew Takieddin went with them.*

*These too struggled to get up the slope, with no better success. It was now nearly midday and the August heat of the Orontes Valley beat upon them, burning down from a cloudless sky, striking up from the rocks beneath, making their arms a burden to them and exhausting their strength. By midday the second division began to retire and Saladin went out to meet them and urge them back, at the same time calling up the third division, which had been sitting waiting. The situation of the Franks was now desperate. The weight of their arms and armour, the fierce heat, the activity they must use to compensate for their fewness, began to tell upon them. By now, too, ʿImad-ad-Din's division had been rested, and joined the third and what remained of the second in the continued assault. Losing courage and feeling no longer able to hold them off, the Franks began to retire to the citadel. The Saracens seized their advantage: rushing up the slope they managed to scale the wall and fight their way into the citadel with the defenders. At the same time a party of Saracens which had been waiting on the eastern slope, either because they had been sent there or because they preferred that part, finding that the concentration of the defence upon the west had left that side bare of defenders, scaled it and were soon inside. Once in the lower bailey, the same cause enabled them to make their way into the upper, which they entered at the same moment as the melée of Franks and Saracens from the other side. The Franks made their way back to the donjon, but they were exhausted and heavily outnumbered. The cries of their Moslem prisoners finally caused them to think that the donjon, too, had been entered, and they submitted.*[32] The lady of Bourzey, who fell into Saladin's hands and was at once released, was a sister of the second wife of Bohemund of Antioch, Sibylla, a woman of dubious character, generally suspected of being in secret communication with the Moslems. Antioch itself was spared, for another seventy years of insecurity.

ANTIOCH TO
ALEPPO

The most dangerous point in Antioch's defences had always been the open country, traversed by an old Roman road, that led to Aleppo. Twenty-five miles east of Antioch was the castle of Harim occupied by the crusaders in 1086 and lost by them in 1164. On an isolated mound, covered by a great stone glacis, the castle, of which little now remains, is Arab work of the late twelfth and thirteenth centuries, and must in its completeness have rivalled the great citadel of Aleppo.

To the north the route to Alexandretta led through the Amanus mountains by the pass of Beylan. This was the way by which reinforcements would come, and in 1188 Saladin neglected the reduction of Antioch itself to secure the castles guarding this approach; Baghrās and Darbsāk. Both these castles were held by the Templars, who resisted resolutely, but both capitulated when their appeals for help from Antioch received no reply. Darbsāk, on an oval hilltop, was a comparatively small fortress still

BAGHRĀS
*See page 58*

probably mainly Byzantine in its workmanship. Baghrās was a very different matter, and still in its secluded valley is an impressive ruin, a compact, forbidding block. Byzantines, Franks, Armenians, and Mamluks have contributed to its present form, though the greater part of the masonry shows the small stones of Armenian builders. On a steep hillock, which requires no separating ditches, the inner enceinte still towers above the outer wall.

ARMENIAN
CASTLES

Beyond the confines of Antioch, on the southern slopes of the Taurus mountain and the coastal strip, was the kingdom of the Armenians, the name assumed by Leo II when he was crowned in 1198. For a hundred years previously the Armenians, originally refugees from the Selchükid conquests in the high tableland between Lake Van and the Black Sea, had been occupying strongpoints and playing off their neighbours, Byzantium, Crusaders, and Turks, against one another. Leo II, who reigned till 1219, was a great builder, and many of the ruined fortresses still partially standing must date from his time. Few of them have any documented history. At Anazarba, the rectangular castle on the narrow col joining the two enceintes has an inscription dated to 1188, and the fortifications include some stretches of Byzantine wall and some Arab rebuilding after its capture by Hārūn al-Rashīd in 796. This re-use of earlier work is characteristic of the Armenian castles, and their precipitous sites had already attracted Byzantine or brigand occupation. Nature rather than art protects them, but their

Island fortress at Le Courc (Corycus)

small, regular masonry, roughly bossed, and their projecting horseshoe towers are easily recognizable features. One or two of them were for a time held by the Templars, Hospitallers, or princes of Antioch. At Sarvantikar, in Antiochene hands from 1185 to 1194, the keep may be Frankish work. At Camardesium above Silifke on the sea plain, the fineness of the masonry and the vaulting suggest that the SILIFKE Hospitallers, to whom it was ceded in 1210, must have brought some of their own masons with them, but its great horseshoe towers are Armenian in inspiration. At Tall Hamdun (Toprakkale), another Hospitaller holding, at the eastern entrance to the Cilician plain, the rounded towers rise as at Krak from a talus faced with masonry. Lampron, north of Tarsus, was the centre of a powerful fief, and its two towers still jut out upon overhanging rocks, which have been cut away to increase their steepness. Tumlu, a castle identifiable in the chroniclers, crowns an equally precipitous outcrop. Visible from it, the castle of Yilan has a series of three wards at different levels on its rocky hill, with two splendid YILAN towers defending its gateway. Vagha controls a lesser pass in the Anti-Taurus mountains. Paperon from its isolated rock looks across the Cilician plain towards the sea at Mersina and to the north to the snow-capped encircling height of the Taurus mountains. At Le Courc (Corycus: Gorigos) there is an CORYCUS island fortress built according to an inscription in 1151, joined at one time by a causeway to a land citadel, which incorporates a Roman gateway and a tower with a classical doorway. On the western point of the Armenian coastal plain Anamur is the most complete of all the castles, with thirty-six ANAMUR towers standing, its inner ward over-topping its outer sea defences, an immensely impressive group of buildings, an undisturbed setting for the middle ages, though much of its present state is Turkish rebuilding.[33]

EDESSA The county of Edessa, occupied in 1098, lost in 1144, seems to contain few memorials of its crusading rule, but separated from Syria by the modern Turkish frontier it has been somewhat inaccessible and its medieval remains have not been exhaustively examined. Edessa (Urfa) itself is mainly Byzantine. Its rock moat, 500 feet long with an average depth of 60 feet and a width of 30 feet, has a pinnacle left standing as a bridge pier, similar, though on a smaller scale, to that of Saone. At Rum Qal'at, on the most westerly bend of the Euphrates, the ramp passes through a succession of gates, and a great moat was cut in the hillside, but the fortifications, which include some Armenian work, are probably of very various dates. Tall Bashir (Turbessel) is entirely laid waste. Bira (Birejik), the Frank castle on the Euphrates which defied the siege of Zengi in 1145, has been mainly rebuilt by az-Zāhir Ghāzi and its most conspicuous features are Arab work. Lower down the river, Qal'at Najm, the great castle built with blocks of smooth ashlar, is also az-Zāhir's work.

RHODES, ETC. Outside of Palestine and Syria, in Cyprus, in Rhodes, and on the mainland of Greece, the crusading endeavour was to continue and castles were to be built by them. At Rhodes and at Budrum, the site of Halicarnassus, the knights of St. John were to continue their tradition and be pioneers in new methods of fortification as medieval walls ceased to resist artillery bombardment. Elsewhere, in Greece and many of the islands, the work is on a lesser scale, and does not equal the achievements of the crusading kingdom and its master builders.

The castle of Anamur. See page 81

Baptistery on the north wall of the Church at Gibelet (Jubail). See page 93

# THE CHURCHES

Outside of Jerusalem, the church of most compelling sanctity was that of Bethlehem. The basilica as the crusaders found it, and as, in its main structure it exists today, dates from Justinian's times, much of it raised on Constantinian foundations.[1] There was little need for alteration and rebuilding, and the crusading work was confined to the monastic buildings for the community of Augustinian canons, whom they installed as custodians of the church, now become a Latin cathedral. In 1948–51 the cloister, which had been walled up, was restored and its simple Gothic arcade, with double colonnettes and stiff leaf capitals, can once more be appreciated. But, if the main structure was retained, within it a decorative scheme was carried out on a scale which equalled that in the Holy Sepulchre and which partially survives today. An inscription, the Greek version of which is still extant, the Latin known from earlier records, states that *the present work was finished by the hand of Ephrem the monk, painter and mosaic worker, in the reign of the Great Emperor Manuel Porphyrogenitus Comnenus and in the time of the great King of Jerusalem, our Lord Amalric, and of the most holy bishop of holy Bethlehem, the Lord Ralph, in the year 6677, second indiction (1169)*. Here then are works of art closely linked with a political situation. Amalric in 1169 married Manuel's niece, Maria. There were plans for close co-operation between Jerusalem and Constantinople; Manuel was even discussing a possible re-union of the churches; the adroit and popular bishop Ralph, for so William of Tyre describes him, seems to have made use of the opportunity both of redecorating his church and of giving a concrete manifestation of the alliance. These inscriptions are in the apse of the choir, and we know that the transepts had mosaics of the life of Christ and of the Virgin, following fairly normal Byzantine iconography in the choice of subjects. Of these, blackened and fragmentary patches on the wall, the Incredulity of St. Thomas and the Entry into Jerusalem are relatively complete, the Transfiguration and the Ascension partially but recognizably visible. They must have been of high quality, more elaborate in their settings than the slightly later series at Monreale in Sicily, the only comparison near in date; and with some unusual details, such as the movement of Christ, taking St. Thomas' hand to guide it to the wound in His side.

In the crypt, above the traditional site of the manger, is a mosaic of the Nativity. Long obscured by dirt and hidden by curtains, it was cleaned in 1944. Much has fallen away, but enough remains to show its vivid colouring in which a rich blue predominates and to confirm that the design was the familiar Byzantine one of the Madonna recumbent, behind her the ox and ass, the Child at her side, the shepherds on her left hand receiving the message of the angel, Joseph on her right, and below the midwives preparing the bath.

In the nave the mosaic decoration is continued on the north wall by representations of the seven oecumenical councils and six provincial ones, Carthage, Laodicea, Gangrae, Sardica, Antioch, and Ancyra, symbolized by altars set in arcades divided by foliage patterns. The absence of human figures may have preserved them from Moslem iconoclasm. The provincial councils are labelled in Greek and it is generally thought that they represent a much earlier eighth-century scheme, stylistically parallel to the Umaiyad decoration of Damascus and the Dome of the Rock. The Franks added opposite to them the oecumenical councils, which, more meagre in ornament, are labelled in Latin; and on both sides, below the councils, friezes with the heads of Christ's ancestors. Above, between the clerestory windows, they placed a procession of angels, of which six survive, figures of great elegance and distinction, advancing with outstretched hands towards the choir and the actual place of the Nativity, their curved postures echoed in the flow of their drapery. On one of these angel panels occurs the name in Latin script, Basilius Pictor, a name which we shall meet again in another context. The letters B. S. also appear on the oecumenical council of Constantinople, possibly again the painter's signature, and, if so, a further indication that the councils of the south wall were twelfth-century work.

Mosaic was not the only form of figure representation. On the upper portions of the pillars of the nave were painted figures of prophets and saints; these were much blackened by dirt, but were cleaned and photographed in 1946. The subjects can be identified from names given in Latin, in a few instances in Latin and Greek, beside the figures; some also have appropriate texts in either language. In some cases large patches of paint have disappeared; the faces are mostly worn very thin; but owing to their height from the ground and the continuous Christian occupation of the church they have been little mutilated. It seems more as if the pillars had been cleaned on some occasion with no regard for the paintings, though at some other date an attempt appears to have been made to preserve them by applying coats of varnish. John Mariti in 1767 described them as *pitture dei secoli barbari,* covered with dust, and thought that the marble columns would have looked better without them. The paint used is some fairly thick medium, possibly mixed with oil. It is not fresco or tempera, though some of the finer details, now gone, may have been worked in the latter medium. To William of Tyre painting was a familiar process from which in the introduction to his history he draws a simile for his own work and the use others might make of it: *those who are inexperienced in painting and not yet admitted to its secrets are allowed to trace out the first design and apply the rough colours, while later the hand of a more skilled artist adds with nobler colours the finishing touches of beauty.*[2] Such was doubtless the procedure at Bethlehem. The saints chosen are very various, and suggest no iconographical scheme but rather a series of votive paintings, and under three of them are kneeling donors in the pointed cloaks and close-fitting tunics of the mid-twelfth century. One of the paintings has the date 15 May 1130, but it is probable, given their stylistic variations, that they were painted at various times.

WALL-PAINTINGS  The few remains of crusading wall-painting provide little comparison with those at Bethlehem. In the crypt of a small church at Sebastia, further up the hill above the cathedral, there are some traces of painting where still can be deciphered the decapitation of the Baptist and the finding of his head, said to have been hidden by Salome at this site: the church of Abū-Ghosh has some figures of saints: in the small church of St. Phocas at Amyūn there are figures painted on the columns, but this, though possibly a twelfth-century church, was dedicated to a Greek saint, and its paintings with their Greek inscriptions are entirely Byzantine. Recently (1965) in clearance work at the Damascus Gate in Jerusalem the foundations of a small crusading chapel were excavated, and some of the masonry still retains its plaster and painted covering, decorative roundels, and a fragment of drapery from some figure, where the long pointed folds, outlined in white along the edges, are closely related to the handling of similar folds at Bethlehem. Certainly wall-painting was a not uncommon practice, and there is evidence enough that a local school of painters was available for the work.

CHURCH AT HEBRON  The crusaders were, as befitted the impulse that had sent them forth, active church builders. Some of these churches were adaptations of earlier buildings. At Hebron the massive enceinte with its huge masonry is a Herodian construction; the church was based on Byzantine foundations but altered to carry twelfth-century groined vaults. Hebron was in 1119 the scene of a striking incident. The patriarchs, Abraham, Isaac, and Jacob, were known to have been buried in vaults under the mosque that had now been occupied and was being rebuilt by Augustinian canons. Beneath two small, probably Umaiyad, cupolas two eyeholes (one of which is still open) looked down into indeterminate caverns. To the Latins the relics of the patriarchs were an inviting trove. Researches were undertaken and eventually, after various disappointments, a well-built tomb chamber was opened containing bones which were acclaimed as those sought for. Some seventeen years later an account was drawn up based on the narratives of participants. It is one of the earliest reports of an excavation. The caves have long been closed: the mosque itself is still somewhat difficult of access and no unbeliever may explore its lower regions. In 1917, when the English occupied the town, an officer, investigating the enclosure, penetrated into a subterranean chamber which held what seems to have been some form of tomb slab, but he had no knowledge of the archaeological interest of the spot where he found himself nor did the circumstances of the moment permit of any close examination.[3]

Of the smaller churches, the general pattern was a nave with aisles ending in three apses, set in a RAMLA rectangular chevet. Ramla provides a well preserved example, little altered by its conversion to a mosque. Nearby, the church of St. George at Lydda is probably, to judge from its capitals, slightly LYDDA later in date. It was destroyed by Saladin and a hundred years later Baybars used some of the material to build a bridge nearby, a bridge which is still in use. Only the central and northern apses survive, embodied in a church built in 1874 by the Orthodox Greeks. The workmanship is outstandingly good and the crusading church, as befitted the shrine of St. George, must have been a notable building.

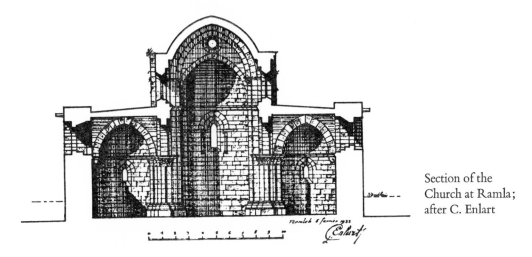

Section of the
Church at Ramla;
after C. Enlart

The church of Qariet al-ʿInab, the possible site of Emmaus, more generally known from a nine- EMMAUS teenth century brigand occupier as Abū-Ghosh, has had a singularly varied history. Built on the (ABŪ-GHOSH) foundations of a fort of the tenth Roman legion, it had the normal twelfth-century form of nave, aisles, and triple apse. The transverse arches of its groin vaults are supported on bent angle consols, the same that are found in the cloisters of the Holy Sepulchre, the cathedral at Ramla, and on the façade of the Aqṣa mosque, where they may be of Arab workmanship. Its walls were frescoed with paintings, now very fragmentary, but which were carefully described by Charles Virolleaud in 1923, when much more was visible. Byzantine in iconography and style, they had Latin inscriptions, and, as at Bethlehem, figures were painted on the pillars. When taken by the Saracens in 1187, it must have been one of the most carefully ornamented of the minor churches. For a brief period in the fifteenth century, the Franciscans were allowed to reoccupy it, but in 1489 or 1490 it was overrun by a band of robbers who burned alive the nine Franciscans they found there. From then on it was a brigand stronghold, though Abū-Ghosh himself, a friend of Lady Hester Stanhope and impressive host to Lamartine, deserves perhaps a more distinguished title. In 1901, thanks to the initiative of the Marquis de Vogüé, it was handed over to some French Benedictines and a thorough restoration was undertaken.

87

Abū-Ghosh was an Hospitaller foundation. Ramla and Lydda were combined as a bishopric under the patriarchate of Jerusalem. The organization of the Latin Church in the Kingdom was partially planned in Rome, partially based on Greek Orthodox divisions, and partially opportunist, following

GAZA  the course of events. As well as Ramla-Lydda, Bethlehem, Hebron, and Gaza were suffragan sees of the patriarchate: at the last of these the cathedral was hit by a shell in the English artillery bombardment of 1916, when it was being used as a munitions store, and the minaret, built on the eastern apses, fell, destroying part of the nave. The church has been restored, and the western doorway, with its crocket capitals, was undamaged. Inside, the piers have attached semi-columns, which seem to be re-used Byzantine work, and there are similar semi-columns standing on the cornice of the piers. The whole elevation, hardly a satisfactory one, seems based on the sizes of columns available. Another casualty

IBELIN  of the 1914–18 war was the church at Ibelin, where only a doorway with some godron voussoirs now survives. Here, as at Lydda, stones were taken to build a bridge.

Three archbishoprics were dependent on the patriarchate: Caesarea, Nazareth, Tyre; and Petra (La

KERAK  Pierre du Désert). Of this last little is known. The intrepid naval officers, Irby and Mangles, describe a church at Kerak: *The most remarkable thing that we observed was a Christian church, within the enceinte of this part of the castle; it is very ill constructed with small stones, and some pillars are laid horizontally into the masonry, forming quite a contrast to the Mahommedan work, which is of large well cut stones, laid in regular courses. The church has small narrow windows and a circular end and arched front. There are remains of paintings of large groups of figures on the stuccoed walls; one seems to have represented a king in armour, another the martyrdom of some saint by twisting out his bowels; and there is an imperfect inscription with letters of the Gothic form.*[4] This may well have been the most important church of the area.

CAESAREA  The cathedral of Caesarea, rebuilt on the site of a Byzantine church, must have been a notable building, though one that suffered much in this fought-over city. Baybars destroyed Caesarea very effectively in 1268, and Burchard when he visited it in 1280 describes it as *altogether ruined. At this place,* he writes, *I fell into very great danger, but the Lord of His mercy saved me.* It is only in recent years that Israeli excavations have begun to explore this site, and to add considerably to our knowledge of it.

SEBASTIA  Caesarea had only one suffragan bishopric, that of Sebastia, the ancient Samaria. Here, building on foundations and in places the lower courses of a Byzantine church, the crusaders raised, over the reputed tomb of the Baptist, a large church, 150 feet long by 75 broad.[5] No documents or mentions by chroniclers give information as to its dates or builders, but it must have been completed before Saladin took the town in 1187. Theodoric, a German pilgrim, in 1172 described how the Baptist was buried between Elisha and Obadiah in a crypt reached by thirty-four steps: he was careful to state that the head was at Constantinople and that the body had been burned by Julian the Apostate, but John Phocas, a Cretan, visiting it five years later, says that his ashes were contained in an urn and his left hand in a golden case, and that his parents, Zacharias and Elisabeth, were also buried there. Neither author describes the church, though it must then have been in course of construction or very recently completed. In 1187 Saladin captured the city and it remained in Arab hands. Burchard of Mt. Sion in 1283 describes how the cathedral has become a mosque. He, as Theodoric a hundred years before him, wondered at the great Herodian ruins that crowned and still crown the hill, and moralized over so great a city come to such wretchedness. When Léon de Laborde drew it in 1827 the central apse, though ruined, was still standing, and, unusually in the crusading kingdom, it was polygonal in form, projecting beyond those of the aisles, instead of being enclosed in a flat east end. But everything is unusual at Sebastia. There was no cupola over the crossing, and the vaults were carried on ribs rising alternately from composite piers and twin pillars. Enough remains to show the excellence of the masonry, laid without cement, and the faultless early Gothic style of the capitals. Here is work that must have been supervised by experienced Western builders, with Western carvers available to work for them. Earlier work, however, may have been both more Romanesque and less skilled. The museum of Constantinople has four capitals, taken from this church in 1897: carved on two sides, they seem to have come from a doorway, and a scene of dancers and musicians suggests that they illustrated the story of the Baptist; on one of them volute heads emerge from late Romanesque foliage. In their heavy figures, relieved by considerable use of the drill, they resemble two capitals which were found in Damascus but whose original provenance is not known. On each of the Damascene capitals there is a mounted warrior, whose iconographical significance, sometimes interpreted as Constantine triumphing over paganism, remains uncertain. They may well have come from the Sebastia area.

Two other churches nearby deserve some notice. At Nablus the church of the Resurrection, begun NABLUS in 1167, had an elaborate doorway, fairly complete until the earthquake of 1927, and, amongst its stiff leaf foliage, the most developed Palestinian example of this style, an odd scene of a symbolic lamb between a mermaid and a lion had surprisingly escaped mutilation. A mile outside the town the crusaders rebuilt a Byzantine church over the well of Jacob, the scene of Christ's meeting with the Samaritan woman. Ruined in 1187, and at various times rebuilt by the Orthodox Greeks, it is still possible to see that in its use of alternate pillars and columns it resembled the cathedral of Sebastia. Unusually for the Kingdom, it seems to have had projecting transepts.

Nazareth, the scene of the Annunciation and the childhood of Christ, had high claims on crusading NAZARETH devotion, and a Russian pilgrim, the Abbot Daniel, as early as 1106–7 describes *a great and high church* there, built over the grotto which was shewn as the dwelling place of Mary, where the angel appeared to her, though the Orthodox Greeks supported the account in the Gospel of St. James and had built their church in the twelfth century by the village fountain.[6] There was also a crusading church on the site supposed to be that of the workshop of St. Joseph. Canon Jean Doubdan, who went on pilgrimage in 1651, was much exercised by these ambiguities, to which was added the problem of the position of the Virgin's house before its miraculous transference to Loreto. *That detestable heresiarch Luther,* he impatiently ends up, *says that the Angel announced the Mystery of the Incarnation to this Queen of Angels as she went one fine morning to draw water from this fountain… but this is mere imagining.*[7]

Nazareth in the twelfth century was presided over by Archbishop Letard, who was elected in 1158, having previously been prior, and was still living in 1181. William of Tyre describes him as *a very kindly man, gentle and affable.* It was under his rule that the extension and elaboration of the church of the Annunciation was undertaken. It was a large building, 244 feet long by 98 broad, consisting of a nave and two aisles. The side apses were encased in a rectangular outer wall from which the central apse, also rectangular on the exterior, projected to some distance. Of the twelve piers of the nave, eight were square, four polygonal; the surviving capital of a small column, probably from a composite pier, is a finely carved acanthus with a grinning mask between the volutes. The excavations carried out by Father Prosper Viaud in 1907 immensely increased our knowledge of the building and revealed the high quality of the masonry. As the work was nearly over, the most remarkable find took place. A small rock-cut chamber, such as is common in Nazareth, was penetrated and, covered with debris, five capitals were discovered. Carved with scenes from the lives of the apostles, unweathered and only here and there chipped, the Nazareth capitals are splendid examples of Romanesque art. It is clear from their state that they had never been placed in position, and must have been hidden away when in 1187 it was certain that the Moslems would capture the town. Iconographically they are of considerable interest, representing, by the most probable interpretation, scenes from the lives of St. Peter, St. Thomas, St. James, St. Matthew, and St. Bartholomew. Peter and James are saints with strong local connexions in Palestine, and the healing of Tabitha at Jaffa, and the execution of St. James at Jerusalem are subjects which could be easily expected. The other three apostles are the missionaries of India, of the East which Gervase of Tilbury divides into *India superior* (St. Bartholomew), *India inferior* (St. Thomas), and *India meridiana* (St. Matthew). The whole programme foreshadows the missionary journeys eastward of the following century. Certainly they were carved on the spot, for the stone is a local yellow sandstone; the capitals are incompletely worked, and the backgrounds to the figures have never been cut to a smooth finish. There has been much use of a drill, and there is deep undercutting. The drapery forms round whorls and swinging curves, such as are familiar in the high Romanesque art of Western Europe. Deschamps has shewn that their markedly individual style, the long-nosed facial type, the drapery with its drilled ornament, the dramatic sense of gesture, the emaciated, feathered devils are all found on a capital of the Temptation of Christ in the church of Plaimpied near Bourges. The stylistic agreement is such that it is hard not to believe that the Plaimpied sculptor came to Palestine with the second crusade and continued his work there, and the dates fit well with such a thesis.[8] Whether it were he or some fellow mason of his school, the sculptor of Nazareth is one of the great masters.

In 1955 it was decided to pull down the baroque church that since 1730 had occupied part of the crusading site in order to build a new and larger one. This allowed of, and in fact necessitated, much wider excavations, in the course of which were found another, but much battered, capital and the lower half of an almost life-size figure carved in high relief. Both seem to have been wilfully mutilated, and if, as seems possible, they were part of another cache of sculpture, it was one that was discovered by the iconoclastic enemy.

The finding of this large-scale relief, undoubtedly of the same workmanship as the capitals, raises the question of the position for which these carvings were designed. The slab on which it is cut could hardly have been adjusted to a column, and it would have been surprising to find column figures in use in Nazareth in the 1180's. It could well, however, have been on the side of a doorway as at Moissac or Souillac. Unfortunately, with the upper portion of the figure missing, it is impossible to distinguish its sex, but it is most probably a prophet or apostle. Of the five capitals first found (the sixth is too damaged for certainty), four are octagonal with two faces uncarved, as though for some angle setting, the fifth is four-sided with a circular base and could well have topped the trumeau of a doorway. Its subject, where a crowned and cross-bearing female figure leads a haloed figure away from attacking demons, must be Faith or the Church guiding an apostle, and would be a suitable central incident for the whole iconographic scheme. The problem is complicated by the existence in the Museum of the Greek Patriarchate at Jerusalem of two bearded heads, carved in one block and set at an angle to one another, which is said to have come from Nazareth and which stylistically is from the Nazareth workshop. Here once again the work is incomplete and has never been set in position. What final design was intended must remain speculation, but had it ever been completed it would in quality have rivalled the greatest products of the West.

One other fragment is associated with the group. In the Duke of Devonshire's collection at Chatsworth there is the headless figure of a prophet: one hand, much chipped and flattened, carries a scroll, the other gathers the drapery across the breast; the round whorls, patterned neckband, close pleats, and modelling of the neck, all strikingly recall the Nazareth workshop. It came to the collection with a Hellenistic figure of Diana and the provenance of the two fragments was thought to be *the mountainous country between the coasts of Tyre and Sidon and the river Jordan*.[9] The stone is a hard, yellowish limestone,

Above: Details from a capital from the Church of the Annunciation at Nazareth. Below: Torso from Nazareth in the Duke of Devonshire's collection at Chatsworth

91

not unlike that of Nazareth. The torso now stands 41 inches high; that recently found at Nazareth, cut off at the waist line, measures 33 inches. It is coarser work than that of the Nazareth pieces, by a lesser hand, but its stylistic connexion is unmistakable. It was either part of the final design, by a less able carver, or some derivative from it. The relief that Pococke saw in 1738 of Judith cutting off the head of Holofernes, which must surely have been a decapitation of the Baptist, may well have belonged to this same series. In the strange history of the crusades the activity of this Nazarene mason's yard is one of the most notable artistic events.

TIBERIAS

Nazareth had only one suffragan see, that of Tiberias, and here the crusading church has left no trace. The town still had, as shewn in drawings, a complete circuit of walls in 1837, possibly enclosing medieval buildings, but a severe earthquake of that year overthrew walls and houses and reduced the castle, much altered from crusading times, to a heap of ruins. *Le tremblement de terre de 1837,* wrote de Vogüé in 1872, *n'a laissé debout à Tibériade que quelques massures où des Juifs attendent le Messie dans les cloaques peu forts pour l'attirer.* Since then a gradual process of rebuilding has produced an undistinguished modern town, within the ruined circuit where Herodian masonry still recalls its greater days.

TYRE

The great cathedral of Tyre was built on the site and with some of the materials of the Byzantine church where Origen was buried, his tomb built into the wall of the church. *I have seen his monument there,* wrote Burchard, and added *there are pillars of marble and other stone of such a size that one is astonished at the sight of them.* Two of these pillars now lie derelict, played over by the children of this small village that has succeeded to so much ancient greatness. The cathedral, almost as large as that at Nazareth, ended in three semicircular apses, whose ruins survived late enough to be photographically recorded. It was the burial place of the bones of the Emperor Frederick Barbarossa, and the scene in 1874 of the slightly ludicrous excavations of Professor Sepp in search of them. Nothing now remains except the fallen columns, and a clutter of houses covers much of the site. *But this once famous Tyrus is now no other than an heap of ruins; yet have they a reverent respect, and do instruct the pensive beholder with their exemplary frailty.* So wrote George Sandys in 1612; today some modern houses, some glimpses of walled gardens, give a certain charm to the small fishing port on its peninsula, and nearby excavation is unearthing some of its ancient glory, but it remains a place of memories, a shadow of a name.

Six bishoprics depended from it: Acre, Sidon, Beirut, Gibelet, Tripoli, and Tortosa, the last three being much disputed between the patriarchs of Antioch and Jerusalem. Of these sees only three now have crusading churches of any completeness. The cathedral of St. John the Baptist at Beirut survives BEIRUT as a mosque, and its triple rounded apses, with on the exterior applied columns as buttresses and a series of carved metopes, is as good a piece of Romanesque architecture as any that survives in Syria. The little cathedral of Gibelet is a poorer building, chiefly notable for a flaw in its alignment, the axis GIBELET<br>*See page 84* of the nave having been altered from that of the apses. The chevet, modelled on that of Beirut, is circular, but without the column buttresses and much less richly carved. There is however one feature of considerable charm and interest, the small domed baptistery built on the north wall, with open arches elaborately decorated with chevrons, rosettes, dog tooth, and godrons and crowned with a carved cornice.

TORTOSA

Of all the crusading essays in Gothic, the cathedral of Tortosa is the most satisfactory. Maundrell described it in 1697: *It is one hundred and thirty foot in length, in breadth ninety three, and in height sixty one. Its Walls, and Arches, and Pillars, are of a Bastard Marble, and all still so entire, that a small expence would suffice to recover it into the state of a beautiful Church again. But, to the grief of any Christian Beholder,*

Opposite page:
Tortosa Cathedral,
by William Bartlett.
From an engraving

*it is now made a stall for Cattle, and we were, when we went to see it, almost up to our knees in Dirt and Mire.*[10] Some hundred and forty years later when William Bartlett drew it, little had changed in its condition. Then in 1851 it, at long last, became a mosque, but by 1914 it was once more derelict and was taken over as a Turkish barracks. In 1922 some repairs were carried out; now, in very recent years, it has become a museum, filled with display cases, lacking some of its old romance, *imprégné de roman* René Dussaud called it in 1927, but assured of reasonable preservation.

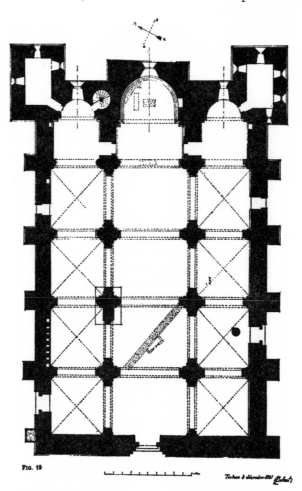

Plan of the Cathedral of Tortosa; after C. Enlart

FIG. 19

    Tradition had it that St. Peter had dedicated here the first church in honour of Our Lady, and a small compartment, arranged in one of the pillars of the nave may mark some ancient shrine. No document gives indication as to the date of the building, but there is a clearly marked division on the north wall after the second bay and on the south after the third. The façade and the western bays are Gothic rather than Romanesque in detail, and a new building stone was used. Expert masons were employed in both building periods, and the style of the earlier capitals suggest that they must date from before Saladin's capture of the town in 1188 or from some immediate rebuilding shortly after it, when the pilgrimage began to revive in popularity. They provide a whole repertory of foliage forms, from the flat, veined acanthus, to the plain rounded leaf, placed first in two parallel rows, then spreading luxuriantly over the whole capital, with small human masks between the volutes. In the thirteenth-century work, over the old outline of the acanthus, flowers and petalled leaves cluster into projecting crockets, almost ready to break away into naturalism, but still restrained by the old formal convention.

Interior of the Cathedral of Tortosa (Tartūs)

Beside one capital of the upper windows of the façade, the sculptor has carved a jackal, such as those that of an evening come close to the towns and villages of Syria. The façade, now deprived of its doorway, which was probably torn out for the marble or fine stone composing it, must always have been severe, and its fortress-like effect was increased by its two square towers. *I entreated the king,* Joinville writes, *to allow me to go on pilgrimage to Notre Dame de Tortosa, which was a great resort of pilgrims, because the first altar that was ever built in honour of the Mother of God upon earth was there.*[11]

Capital in the Cathedral of Tortosa; after C. Enlart

ACRE     Acre has little left to recall the century when it was the capital of the Kingdom and one of the great markets of the Levant. Ludolph of Suchem, a German Franciscan, who visited it some forty years after its loss, gives us the tradition, then still lively, of its past splendour. *I must say somewhat about this city of Acre; yet when I think of its present state I had liefer weep than say anything. ... The streets within the city were exceedingly neat, all the walls of the houses of like height with one another and built without exception of hewn stones, being wondrously adorned with glass windows and painting. Moreover, all the palaces and houses of the city were built not simply to serve ordinary needs, but designed with a care for human comfort and enjoyment, being fitted up inside and decorated outside with glass, painting, hangings and other ornament, as each man was able. The public places of the city were covered over with silken sheets or other splendid stuffs for shade. At every street corner stood a very strong tower protected by an iron door and chain. The nobility lived round the inner part of the city in exceedingly strong castles and palaces. In the centre of the city lived the craftsmen and merchants, every one in a special place according to his trade, and all the inhabitants of the city deemed themselves like the Romans of old and carried themselves like noble lords, as indeed they were. ... There also resided in Acre the richest merchants under heaven, who had come together out of every nation; there dwelt the Pisans, Genoese and Lombards, through whose cursed strife the city was brought low; for they likewise carried themselves as lords. Not only the richest merchants but the most diverse folk dwelt there, for from the rising to the setting of the sun all kinds of wares were brought hither; all the strange and rare things which are to be found in the world were brought thither on account of the nobility and princes who themselves resided therein.*[12] No doubt the memories of this golden age are overcharged, but the immense prosperity of Acre, hemmed in as it was by hostile neighbours, is well established and a testimony both to the flow of trade, whatever the disturbances around it, and to the vitality of the crusading stock. It was also a city of churches. The patriarchate had been transferred there; the monks of St. Mary of Jehoshaphat had built a new church and monastery there to replace that which they had lost; dispersed communities made themselves new homes, and the coming of the friars, the Franciscans and the Dominicans, gave a new impetus to religious foundations. St. Francis himself was there in 1219. Peter des Roches, Bishop of Winchester, founded an English hospice, that of the English saint, Thomas the Martyr. Of these churches, practically nothing now remains. Many must have been damaged at the sack of the town in 1291. The church of St. Andrew was the largest and its ruins stood for many years. Corneille le Bruyn drew it in 1681, and shews it to have been a fine Gothic church with five lancet windows on the west façade, surmounted by three oval openings. Round the whole building was a blind arcade of pointed arches. One relic of it survives. Al-Ashraf Khalīl took out its west doorway and transported it to Cairo, where it survives in the tomb mosque of his father, Kalavun. The recession of its columns blends harmoniously with the shallow arches of the mausoleum, and its simple foliage had nothing to offend Moslem susceptibilities. It is a strange survival of the splendours of Acre, but at least has its place in one of the most beautiful of medieval streets. Here and there in the great Cairene mosques other fragments of crusading work can still be found; in the *madrasah* of Sultan Hasan the *mihrab* has twelfth-century Gothic capitals and by the entrance steps, under a great stone rosette of splendid Arab carving, a small column has Romanesque interlaces and three reliefs of buildings, one of which is the Temple, the other two probably the Church of the Sepulchre and Bethlehem.

Both the Templars and the Hospitallers had considerable buildings in Acre. The great hall of the latter order, filled in by the early nineteenth-century rulers of Acre as foundations for their palace and later converted into a prison, has in 1954 to 1956 been cleared of the filling material and can now be seen as a Gothic building with ribbed vaults rising from round pillars. In 1748 the German Franciscan, Ladislaus Mayer, drew the remains of the Templars' house and chapel, with amongst them a graceful oriel window; when he returned four years later it had been levelled to the ground. In these intervening years, the Beduin chief, Daher al-ʿUmar, had made Acre his capital and begun to rebuild it, using the older buildings as a quarry. Civil wars, French and English sieges and the repairs following on them, the monumental ambitions of rulers such as Ahmad Pasha al-Jazzār, nicknamed 'the Butcher', have completed the work. Some vaults in the town are crusading work, but above ground it is all ʿAkkā, and St. Jean d'Acre has disappeared.

Not only building, but other arts flourished. In Jerusalem a scriptorium, presumably that of the Holy Sepulchre, had been producing illuminated manuscripts of high quality, most notably the Melisend Psalter (British Museum, MS. Egerton 1139), which by its obits is closely associated with the royal house of the mid-twelfth century.[13] This is a book which, despite its very English calendar, follows Byzantine prototypes for its illustrations, one of which is signed Basilius, the same name as appears on the mosaics of angels in Bethlehem. It is tempting to associate this work also with the Englishman, Ralph, Bishop of Bethlehem, but there were other possible English influences, such as that of William, prior of the Holy Sepulchre, who became Archbishop of Tyre in 1127, the see where another William, the great historian, was later to succeed him. The influence of the Melisend Psalter must have been considerable, for in a Syriac lectionary (Paris, Bibliothèque Nationale, MS. Syriac 355), which can be dated to between 1193 and 1220, and in another Syriac manuscript of 1222 in the Convent of St. Mark at Jerusalem there is a constant parallelism in the scenes represented and the ornamental borders are similar in type. Melisend, through her mother, Emorfia, had close connexions with the Syrian Christian communities, and here in this interrelationship of the manuscripts is a visual reminder of this particular strand in the complex pattern of the Kingdom.

The Melisend Psalter, still in its ivory covers carved with scenes from the life of David and acts of charity, is a volume made for a royal patron. More normal are two liturgical books, a Sacramentary (divided between the Fitzwilliam Museum, Cambridge, MS. Maclean 49 and the Biblioteca Angelica, Rome, MS. D.7.3) and a Missal (Bibliothèque Nationale, MS. lat. 12056); they have a distinctively Jerusalemite calendar and their figured initials, though related to elements in the Melisend Psalter, are more completely a fusion of Western and Byzantine styles. Enough is now known, thanks to the researches of Dr. Buchthal, to give the art of illumination a high place in crusading artistic achievement.

THE RICCARDIANA
PSALTER

The loss of Jerusalem in 1187 inevitably disrupted such activities, but there are one or two manuscripts which suggest that they were soon resumed. In particular there is a strikingly beautiful Psalter in the Riccardiana Library at Florence (MS. 323). It contains a series of illustrations which, with some omissions, is similar to that of the Melisend Psalter, but used as small rectangular panels in the text, not as full-page designs, though the first two scenes, the Annunciation and the Nativity, are set in a great Beatus page, with David and two prophets filling the straight bar of the B, an admirable piece, richly coloured in dark blues, greens, and purples on a gold ground. Here Western art with subordination of narrative realism to decorative effect triumphs over Byzantinism with its tradition of the framed subject set in a defined space, but the sense of volume and the softness of modelling come from the best Byzantine examples.

By good fortune the manuscript can be approximately dated and the date is by no means an expected one. The Psalter is preceded by a table of solar cycles of twenty-eight years beginning in 1100 and ending in 1212: this suggests strongly that it was written in the fifth cycle, that is between 1212 and 1240, and this is borne out by the table for the computation of Easter which begins in 1230. This notable book is a product of the reoccupation of Jerusalem under Frederick II, and in its high quality and its continuity with earlier Jerusalem work provides an interesting addition to our knowledge of that obscure period. Some of the prayers connect it with a convent of nuns, and the invocations of St. Benedict and St. Anne would point to the convent of St. Anne; that, however, was at this time in Arab hands, and it is likely that the prayers simply repeat those of an earlier volume. More unusual is the inclusion in the list of saints of various patrons of the royal house of England, and there is much to be said for Dr. Buchthal's view that this beautiful work was intended as a gift for Frederick's wife, Isabella, daughter of John of England, whom he married, *en troisièmes noces,* in 1235, a gift sent to Worms for the marriage celebrations by some of Frederick's Palestinian adherents. At the end of the book is a prayer 'pro Comite', who must be John of Brienne, ex-king of Jerusalem, who died in 1137 and who was the father of Frederick's second wife, Yolanda.

ACRE SCHOOL

If the Riccardiana Psalter may well have been produced in Jerusalem during the ten years, 1229 to 1239, of renewed Christian occupation, the real hub of crusading energy was in Acre. Here too fine manuscripts were certainly being illuminated. A Missal in the Capitular Library at Perugia (MS. 6) has the entry on 12 July *Dedicatio ecclesie Aconensis* (that is the cathedral of St. Cross), and this indication of provenance makes it a key piece for the culture of the city. The facial types and some of the gestures are found in other manuscripts, and Dr. Buchthal has built up an impressive corpus of the Acre school, which includes the great mid-thirteenth-century Bible in the Arsenal Library in Paris (MS. 5211) and an equally splendid *Histoire Universelle* in the British Museum (MS. Add. 15268). In the latter manuscript the battle scenes, the Arab musicians, the camel convoys, the canopies and costumes, suggest the life of contemporary Acre, and one subject depicted, the battle with the Amazons, the battle of 'the Queen of Feminie', was we know re-enacted in that great hall of the Hospital, that still survives, by the knights of Acre, clad in women's clothes, at the festivities held in 1286 for the coronation of Henry II, the young, pathetically epileptic, king of Cyprus and Jerusalem, whose coming seemed to bring new hope: and there were *many other games fine and delectable and pleasant.* But in the previous years, Kalavun had captured the fortress of Margat: the net was closing in. Five years later, on 18 May 1291, the Mamluks stormed the walls: the beaches were crowded with fugitives seeking escape to Cyprus, but there were not ships for all, and some that there were sank overladen. The conquerors, massacring in the town, closed down upon the unhappy remnants round the harbour. For a time, till 28 May, the Templars held out in their fortress: then the great tower was mined and fell, crushing alike defenders and assailants.

It is not, however, only in illumination that works of the Acre school survive. In the monastery of Mount Sinai a group of icons were photographed in 1958 and 1960 by a joint expedition of the universites of Michigan, Princeton, and Alexandria, and are at present in course of publication by Professor Kurt Weitzmann.[14] The monastery of Mount Sinai has always been geographically one of the most isolated Christian centres, and since the Moslem conquest of Egypt and Syria it has been surrounded not only by deserts but by a hostile faith. Curiously this exposed position in the end made for its security. Mahomet himself recognized the sacred nature of the site and gave the monastery a writ of protection. This has constantly been renewed by Selchükids, Mamluks, and Ottomans, and, though occasionally raided by Beduin tribes, the monastery has preserved its treasures wonderfully intact, protected by its inaccessibility, or partially protected, from the acquisitiveness of scholars and museums. In its great collection of icons, numbering nearly three thousand, there is a large group that can be associated on very secure stylistic grounds with the Acre school. There are links with the Crucifixion scene in the Perugia Missal and some striking parallels with the Arsenal Bible. Some of these panels are designed to fit in the beam of an iconostasis and carry rather halting inscriptions in Greek, but their stylistic affinities are with the West. Some still have Latin inscriptions; others Latin repainted with Greek. Many crusading graffiti suggest that, despite the distance, visitors from the Kingdom were not infrequent, and if such intercourse seems insufficient to explain the presence of these numerous icons, it is possible that a large consignment of paintings found their way to Sinai after the fall of the crusading capital. Whatever the method of their journey, they remain a convincing proof of the range and standard of this synthesis of Western and Byzantine art that was practised with such ability in the doomed, hectic but not unprosperous years when Acre was both the last mainland outpost and the central market for Western trade with the Near East.

Sack and earthquake have destroyed beyond any recognition the many churches of Antioch: *Man gave the fatal blow and nature consecrated the sentence.* The basilica of St. Peter and St. Paul, dating from the time of Justinian, was the Latin cathedral. This Byzantine building adapted to another rite was characteristic of the confused nature of Antiochene ecclesiastical policy. In 1165 Bohemund III, in deference to his Byzantine negotiations with his brother-in-law, Manuel Comnenos, had enthroned the Orthodox Patriarch, Athanasius II, in the cathedral, while the Latin Patriarch, Aymeri of Limoges, withdrew complainingly to his castle of Cursat. Then in 1170 the whole of northern Syria was devastated by an earthquake in which, with many other buildings, the cathedral of Antioch collapsed in ruins, burying the clergy who were officiating in it at the time and mortally wounding the Greek Patriarch. It was accepted as the judgement of God, and Aymeri was summoned back, while the dying Athanasius was hurried out of the town in a litter. The cathedral itself must have been rebuilt. Twenty years later, the fleshly remains of Frederick Barbarossa were buried there, while his bones were carried towards Jerusalem, only to find an eventual burial at Tyre. But from the slopes of Mount Silpius rock and earth continued to be dislodged on the city below. When in 1895 van Berchem wrote of his climb to the summit, he retained two memories: *that of an incomparable landscape, wide-spread and melancholy, and that of an agonizing enigma: Antioch, how has she disappeared so as to leave no trace on the surface of the soil?*[15]

NORTHERN
BISHOPRICS

Of the dependent bishoprics of the northern patriarchate, Arta and Edessa were only briefly in crusading hands; at the former there was a church or chapel in the fortress but nothing now remains of this border post; in Edessa the octagonal tower of the chief mosque may be early Christian work, and a square tower in the Mosque of Abraham could be a crusading building. The other two bishoprics were Mamistra and Tarsus. The latter still has in the church of St. Paul (now a mosque) a small rectangular aisled building, with alternate pillars and columns. It is crudely constructed but seems to be Western work, possibly the earliest of all crusading churches; and in another mosque the apse can well date from the twelfth century.

Beyond the walled towns and the immediate environs of Jerusalem there were few monastic houses. The military orders replaced the contemplative life, and the constant raids gave non-combatant communities a precarious existence. The Cluniac house on Mt. Tabor, destroyed by Saladin, restored by Frederick II, and finally overthrown by Baybars, was excavated by the Franciscans in the late nineteenth century, and its ground plan shows it to have been a building of some size. Fragments of sculpture, some of excellent quality, suggest that the west door was elaborately ornamented.

BELMONT

Very different was the Cistercian house of Belmont, on a steep hilltop south-east of Tripoli, appropriately solitary and inaccessible and still today inhabited by monks. So remote was it that the Moslems never troubled to destroy it, and allowed some Greek monks to occupy it after the fall of the Kingdom. Even its bell tower, a thing so strongly prohibited by the conquerors, still stands, a small, vaulted cupola on pointed arches, over the severe but solid buildings; though when Maundrell visited it in 1697 the monks were *calling their congregation together, by beating a kind of a tune with two Mallets on a long pendulous piece of plank at the Church door; Bells being an abomination to the Turks.* The good Anglican chaplain to the Factory at Aleppo found the ceremonies he saw somewhat obscure: *Their service consisted in precipitate, and very irreverent chattering of certain Prayers and Hymns to our blessed Saviour, and to the blessed Virgin, and in some dark Ceremonies; the Priest that officiated spent at least one third part of his time, in compassing the Altar, and perfuming it with a pot of Incense, and then going all round the Congregation flinging his Incense-pot backward and forward, and tendring its smoak with three repeated Vibrations to every Person present. ... On both sides of the body of the Church, were seats for the Monks, in the nature of the stalls for the Fellows of Colleges in Oxford; and on each hand of every seat were placed Crutches. These you find in like manner in most Churches of this Country. Their use is for the Priest to lean upon: The Service being sometimes so long, that they cannot well stay it out, without the assistance of such easements; for they are not permitted by their Rubrick to sit down. The younger Monks, who perhaps may have no great occasion for these supporters, do yet delight to use them (as the Spaniards do Spectacles) not for any necessity, but in affectation of gravity.*[16] Belmont with this continuous habitation and this change of rite has naturally been much altered, but its well-faced stone and lack of ornament still reveal a strict adherence to the primitive simplicity of the Cistercian rule under which it was first founded.

Opposite page: Beatus initial from the Riccardiana Psalter (MS. 323, f. 14ᵛ Riccardiana Library, Florence)

Detail from the Creation page in the *Histoire Universelle*, MS. Add. 15628, f. I$^v$, in the British Museum

Doorway at Le Wast

# EAST AND WEST

From the chroniclers, both Western and Arab, from the comparatively meagre surviving documents such as cartularies and registers, from the Assize of Jerusalem, from pilgrims' accounts, from epic poems such as the *Chanson de Jérusalem* and the *Chanson des Chétifs* we can form a picture of the life of the crusading kingdom, of a society adapting itself to a strange climate, differing civilizations, and a precarious frontier existence. The history of William of Tyre is evidence that high literary standards could be reached; the Assize of Jerusalem and the writings of Philip of Novara and John of Ibelin show legalist preoccupations and a political consciousness as enlightened as any in the contemporary West; but there were no great centres of learning, no havens of secluded study in these insecure settlements. Building on the other hand was an essential function: stone walls were their basic protection; churches were the symbol of their endeavours and proof of their sincerity; and if their scriptoria were not employed in copying works of learning, they at least produced some splendidly adorned volumes. There were painters and mosaicists. A major artist such as the Plaimpied Master could emigrate to these disturbed but soul-satisfying territories.

To the popular mind a handful of hallowed dust or a scraping of sacred stone were more significant than architectural designs, however skilfully composed from varying sources. The crusading fusion of Byzantine, Arab, and Western styles had few European copies, few at least where any direct influence can be deduced. The godrons, the bevelled stone voussoirs, that figure so often and have the supreme place on the portal of the Holy Sepulchre were rarely imitated, and are only commonly found in other spheres of Moorish or Arab influence.

A famous group of early twelfth-century French buildings has been associated with the new intercourse with Constantinople. It has been argued that the cupola churches of south-west France, such as Cahors, Périgueux, Angoulême and others, are a direct copying of Byzantine models. Enlart found in them a striking correspondence to a group of churches in Cyprus, and thought that as the bishop of Cahors, Gerard III, had visited the Holy Land in 1109–12 he might, though there is no record of him visiting Cyprus, easily have done so. But, particularly as none of these Cypriot churches is certainly dated, there seems hardly any need to bring them in, as pendentives were in common Byzantine use even if they seldom follow the curve of the dome as smoothly as in Cyprus and Aquitaine. Unlike most Byzantine domes, the Aquitainean churches have no drum between pendentives and dome, and they use also pointed not round arches. A very similar practice is found in the dome of St. Anne's at Jerusalem and in the pendentives of the lantern of the Church of the Holy Sepulchre (though here there is a drum), buildings which are later than the earliest cupolas of Aquitaine and were contemporary with the main French development of the type. Undoubtedly, however, both Aquitaine and the crusading kingdom owe this architectural form to Eastern contacts, and these must have been strengthened by the crusades.

If Byzantine influences were felt independently of the crusading movement, the same is true of Western relations with Islamic art, though it is often difficult to separate the two, for the Arabs themselves borrowed much from Byzantium. Their earliest buildings such as the Dome of the Rock were almost certainly the work of Greek builders, and the heritage of Sassanian and other motifs from Persia and Mesopotamia. which was to play so large a part in the formation of Islamic art, was one in which Byzantium shared. To Western Europe Islam had an approach through Spain, and Islamic metalwork and textiles circulated almost as freely as Byzantine manuscripts and ivories. The influence of woven stuffs was particularly marked. The fabrics themselves were of a quality that the West could not equal and their repute is preserved in terms such as damask (Damascus), fustian (Fustat), muslin (Mosul), taffeta (Persian *taftah*). The designs, some of them Sassanian in origin and used also in Byzantium, were widely popular; their Kufic inscriptions became a favourite if often inappropriate form of decoration; the confronting elephants from the tenth-century oriental silk that wrapped the bones of St. Josse at the saint's church in the Pas-de-Calais inspired several Romanesque capitals; woven Eastern flowers and plants were copied long before they were known to Western gardens; the motif of the winged griffin, of which the bronze in the Campo Santo at Pisa, probably Fatimid eleventh-century work, or the design on the Shroud of St. Siviard at Sens, are examples, had almost certainly been brought westward by the migrating tribes, but its vogue was reinforced by Arab specimens from Spain and Egypt. In Romanesque art the geometric patterns owe something to Arab usage, and even the figure friezes that the Fatimids tolerated seem akin to European treatment. Strangest of all was the two-headed eagle, certainly pre-Islamic in its origin, so much employed in Eastern stuffs and carvings, which became in the twelfth century the emblem of the Selchükid sultans and passed from them, with much else of heraldic significance, including the use of the term 'azure', to the Holy Roman Empire under Louis the Bavarian. Such interchanges must have been intensified by the crusades; but it is intensification only and the influences were known and felt long previously. The wars in Spain were as fruitful in contacts as those in Palestine. Such events as the capture of Lisbon in 1147 or of Silves in 1189 by bands largely composed of seamen from North Germany, Flanders, and England, provided booty of all kinds, some of which was carried back to the victors' homelands. It was from Spain that Moorish architectural detail passed to France and England, and from the Moorish settlements of Sicily and the North African coast that it influenced southern Italy.

THE POINTED ARCH

Greatest and most discussed problem of all in the architectural relations of East and West is that of the pointed arch. Its use was adopted in crusading building with an earlier and greater readiness than in France or England, but direct influence is hard to establish. One instance is supported by some circumstantial evidence, the priory church of Le Wast, near Boulogne. This was founded by Ida, the saintly mother of Godfrey of Bouillon and Baldwin I, after the departure of her eldest son Eustace in 1100 to join his brothers in the Holy Land. It was completed before 1109. Today only the nave exists, with the space between the pillars filled in to make side walls; the arches are pointed, though flatly and hesitantly, the capitals crude, in some cases with only the volutes carved. Apart from the pointed arches, it is normal provincial work of the early twelfth century, except that the west doorway has a curious decoration of jagged cusps, quite unlike north French work, but closely modelled on an Arab pattern such as that found on the Bāb al-Futūh at Cairo. From 1095 to 1096 a crusading embassy spent ten months in the Egyptian capital. Its leader was Pierre le Chambrier; the rest of its personnel is not known, but it is possible that some master mason was among them, possible too that the Egyptians had used the same motif in Jerusalem on some building that has now disappeared.[1]

RIBBED VAULTS

The arches of Le Wast are built some with a keystone, some without; the former was the common Moslem practice, the latter eventually general in the West; but it was some time before such uniformity was reached and in Syria the crusaders used both methods. Ribbed vaults also appear to have Arab priority; but it was probably from Spain that borrowings were made. The ribbed vaults of the choir and transepts of the Church of the Holy Sepulchre are of somewhat uncertain date. The Church was dedicated in 1149 and is therefore a close successor to St. Denis dedicated in 1144. Some of the work on the two buildings must have been contemporary. The crusading ribs however show no close adjustment to their column supports, which might as well have been designed to take a groined vault. Structurally they are of no great importance and, like many early ribs in the West, their purpose was mainly ornamental. They may represent a half-understood attempt to rival the new fashion of Paris. At Sebastia, though the vaults have fallen, the springing of the ribs suggests a more scientific and experienced approach, perhaps the contribution of some mason newly arrived from the West, for there is no intermediate trace in Palestine of crusading experiment with this method.

Another lively controversy as to crusading influences has been that over the development of military architecture. When Rey and others began to plan and publish the castles of Syria, there was a natural tendency to assume that these great monuments had left a considerable impress on Western techniques of fortification and that the crusader kingdom had provided the opportunity not only for assimilation of Byzantine methods but also for independent and inventive experiment. These assumptions have been vigorously rebutted, particularly by T.E.Lawrence, who argued in his brilliant but inevitably superficial thesis that *in the early state of the Latin Kingdom, the period of the private feudatories, the castles erected in Syria were of a purely Western pattern,* and that many of the later Syrian developments were contemporary with or even preceded by similar innovations in France. There is, with the possible exception of Philippe Chinard, the Cypriot employed by Frederick II in Southern Italy, no clear case of an interchange of building personnel nor any documentation that establishes the copying of crusaders' models in the West. The argument therefore, one way or the other, depends on the comparison of stages reached in castle building in the East and in the West. For such a comparison, accurate dating is required and this in most cases is unobtainable. There are individual studies of many Western castles, mainly scattered in the pages of local archaeological journals, and varying much, not only in the author's equipment for the task, but also in the terminology employed. There exists, however, no general corpus of Western fortification: our knowledge is still haphazard, based on certain celebrated examples, while countless existing ruins, to say nothing of possible results of excavation, remain unplanned and uncodified. Comnenian fortification, a parallel development of clear significance, is a relevant matter that has not as yet been thoroughly examined. The question can therefore be stated only in very general terms. At the time of the first crusade, castle building in stone, though well known from many Roman remains and never a practice entirely discontinued, was in the West reaching a new stage of effective use. In particular, schemes of fortification, while retaining outer works of earth and wooden palisades, were being provided with a main strong point or keep in stone masonry. Of these keeps, that of the Tower of London, begun after 1077 and completed by 1097, was probably the most splendid example, but that of Colchester in England and Loches in France date from the closing years of the century and there were other smaller keeps, of which Beaugency provides a wonderfully complete example. From accounts in the chroniclers it is clear that construction in wood still continued. Lambert d'Ardres in a famous passage describes a three-storied wooden castle on a motte surrounded by an artificial lake: Suger tells of the burning of the castle of Le Puiset in the attack on it in 1111 and of its destruction so that only the earthworks were left. The Bayeux Tapestry, which clearly differentiates certain castles in stone from those composed of wooden towers and palisades, shews us the varying practices of the turn of the century.

These keeps were generally built on mounds, surrounded by a ditch, and with one or two outer courts or baileys as additional defended areas. Usually the keep and mound were astride the curtain wall of the bailey, but in some cases, as at Gisors, they occupied a central position inside the bailey walls. Internally the larger towers were divided by a middle wall, and the main hall was on the first floor, where also was the entrance; the vaulted ground floor was only accessible from within. On the exterior the castles were strengthened by flat ribs (at Loches semicircular on flat dosserets) running the whole height of the building. The base was battered slightly, but there was not any elaborately developed glacis. Where the site required it, ditches were cut in the rock and Robert of Torigni describes the castle of Torigni (built c. 1115) as fortified *with lofty towers, very thick walls and deep ditches, which were hewn out in the rocky mountain itself, and surrounded with waters collected in pools.*[2]

The mid-century saw considerable experiment in the shape of the keep, with a view to avoiding the dead ground at the base inevitable with a rectangular corner. Houdan (c. 1130) is a circular building round an interior square, with projecting cylindrical towers; Provins, octagonal with round towers; Gisors, roughly octagonal; Étampes (c. 1160) has a ground plan shaped as a rounded quatrefoil; Orford (1166–71) is internally cylindrical, externally polygonal, with three large rectangular turrets projecting from it; Conisborough, circular with six large projecting buttresses; the keep of Château Gaillard (1197) is cylindrical with a heavy batter and on the inner side a covering spur also battered: this shape is repeated in the tower built by Philip Augustus at Issoudun. Under this king, much occupied with the fortification of territories conquered from the English, the round keep becomes the normal form. The Louvre as designed by him was a rectangular curtain with cylindrical towers, one of which, built on a larger scale, constituted the keep; this scheme can be well seen in his castle of Dourdan (1220). These round keeps were no longer raised on mounds, but built on strong foundations on the same level as the other defences; they were entered at ground level, as the entrance on the first storey had more often hampered the garrison than the attackers. The great tower of Coucy (c. 1240) was the supreme example of this type.

As with the keep so with the curtain wall the increased use of round or semicircular towers is a marked feature of the twelfth century. Few such curtains have however survived intact and unmodified and the stages of work on them are generally undocumented. Loches is a characteristic example: its stone enceinte dates presumably from the first half of the century; it contained small cylindrical towers of little projection; at a later date three much larger towers were added, the ditch deepened, and a stone pier built to support a bridge across it. These greater towers are round but with slight spurs facing the ditch; almost certainly they date from the capture of Loches by Philip Augustus in 1205. In England rectangular towers (as at Framlingham, c. 1190) remained longer in use, though at Conisborough round, solid towers were added to the earlier wall, apparently at the time that the keep was built. In themselves cylindrical towers were nothing new. At Portchester the English had a Roman example of them and the thirteenth-century round towers of Pevensey are probably built on Roman foundations. One of the most famous of walled towns with round towers is Ávila in Spain, and there the walls in their general scheme seem to date from the last decade of the eleventh century. Elsewhere the round tower is found as a primitive form, particularly in hill country, and there are many examples of it, such as the Tour de la Batiaz at Martigny, that may well be twelfth-century work. In the Byzantine empire, they are a marked feature of Comnenian fortification: the Black Tower of Roumeli Hissar is almost certainly, except for its top two storeys, the work of Alexius Comnenus, and the restorations carried out on the walls of the city by Manuel Comnenus have projecting round towers standing almost completely free of the walls. These are examples which must have been noted and discussed by Western builders and must be partially responsible for the increased use of the round form.

<small>ARROW SLITS<br>AND<br>CRENELLATIONS</small> The details of fortification were also being elaborated. It would be difficult in Western Europe within the range of the twelfth century to detect any clear development in the type of arrow slit, though their use in the lower stages of the building seems to become more common. Similarly with crenellations: few survive and it would be hard to generalize as to changes in their disposition. Hoardings of wood and skins, fixed on corbels, were still a common defensive measure, but in the second half of the century stone machicolations sometimes replaced them in the form of arches slightly advanced

from the main walls, so that through the space left the foot of the walls could be controlled. Such arches are found at Niort, built by Henry II, probably in the sixties, and again at Château Gaillard.

Much that has been said above of Western Europe would be true of Syria. The earliest crusader castles had a rectangular stone keep as their main defence work. The masonry was larger and more solid than that commonly found in France and England and dispensed with any form of supporting rib. The central keep within a rectangular curtain, strengthened by corner towers, may have been more frequent: if so, it was not a practice that influenced the West. At Saone, which may be taken as a developed example of the middle years of the century, the great keep astride the curtain is a purely Western scheme; the rock-cut ditch had French parallels, if not on so grand a scale; the round towers are more scientifically placed and have a greater projection than would be expected in a contemporary Western building; the bent entrance of the lower court cannot be exactly paralleled. Were it in France or England Saone would be an impressive landmark; its ditch, which may well be largely Byzantine work, would at any time and place be a remarkable feat; but it would not mark any decisive break with the tendencies already at work and apparent in the West.

In this discussion, pride of place must be given to Château Gaillard. Begun in 1197 by Richard Cœur-de-Lion and pushed to a rapid conclusion, its defences, though they failed to keep out Philip Augustus in 1204, marked a new completeness in Western Europe. Built on a steep hill joined only by a narrow neck to the main ridge, it provided a site very similar to those of Syria. Richard's defences were in the form of a triangular outwork, then a ditch cut in the rock with a bridge to the main bailey; within the latter rose the inner enceinte on an artificial glacis; at the highest point of the hill was the circular keep. These multiple defences were in no way truly concentric and in this respect Château Gaillard falls far short of Krak, but their individual fields of fire were worked out with the greatest precision. The towers were cylindrical with a large projection beyond the curtain. On the inner curtain surrounding the keep the elliptical wall is composed of a series of curved faces so that at every point the glacis at its foot is controlled; the keep, strengthened on its inner side by a spur, has arched machicolations, as at Niort, but here skilfully adjusted to the batter of the wall so as to secure a wide

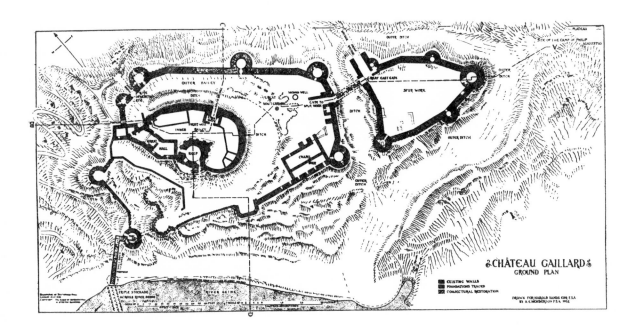

field for the ricochet of any missile discharged through them. The whole building shows a detailed and inventive supervision.

The inevitable question is whether this advance in fortification was due to Richard's crusading experiences. The author of the *Itinerarium* talks with admiration of *the strongly fortified castle of Kyrenia*, but this was not the imposing building that still exists; from the sea Richard saw Margat, where the Hospitallers may at the time have been at work on the great tower, but he did not land till Acre and the castles that he knew were those of the southern coastal plain and the approaches to Jerusalem. Little of them now remains. Athlith had not been built nor Montfort enlarged by the Teutonic knights. The rebuilding of Krak des Chevaliers may have been undertaken and talked of while Richard was in Palestine; arched machicolations, with none of the subtlety of Château Gaillard, had been tried out there in the first building stage before 1170; but Richard never visited the castle. The striped patterning of the outer enceinte of Château Gaillard where the wall is built of alternate courses of brown and white stone, a scheme followed later at Angers, may owe something to an Arab custom that took his fancy, but the science of its planning cannot be exactly traced to any Eastern model and its scheme is still one of relays of defence works rather than a concentric system of supporting fortifications such as characterizes the final form evolved at Krak.

THE CRUSADERS AND ART

In the arts, other than architecture, the crusaders have much to their credit. The Nazareth capitals can equal any Romanesque carvings; the great grille of the Temple is as fine as any surviving medieval iron work; the miniaturists of the Acre school were superb artists. But, if their accomplishment is to be wondered at, nothing they created equalled what they destroyed.

Robert of Clari in his account of the marvels of Constantinople hands down to us the round-eyed wonder of the West at the great luxury and adornment of the Eastern capital: the equestrian statue of Justinian (which he thought to be Heraclius and which survived crusading pillage to be melted down for Turkish cannon); the bronze beasts which crowned the wall of the Hippodrome; the carved columns of Theodosius and Arcadius.[3] To this the sad pendant is the threnody of Niecetas Choniates over the monuments destroyed: the tomb of Justinian broken into and plundered; the bronze Juno of the Hippodrome, whose head could hardly be moved in a cart drawn by four horses, overthrown and broken up, the first victim among the great statues; Paris, offering the apple to Venus, cast from his pedestal; the Hercules, thought to be the masterpiece of Lysimachos, was not respected *though a symbol of human strength, by those who placed strength above all else;* the statue of Helen was burned by the fire, *she who had enflamed so many hearts.* So the mournful catalogue continues of those days which above all others destroyed the heritage of the art of Greece, though had they spared it, it is little likely that it would have survived the still more fatal day of 29 May 1453.[4]

THE VENETIANS

To the Venetians, Byzantine art was a familiar matter, of which their own buildings were no mean branch. They could as merchants appraise the craftsmanship of the objects, and desire them for their own sake. The booty that came to their city was certainly rich and varied and gave new life to Italian Byzantinism at a moment when the Cistercians, the vanguard of the Gothic style, were establishing themselves in the peninsula. Few details are known as to the exact pieces saved as Venetian loot; but above the main portico of St. Mark's stand the four bronze horses, works probably of a Chian sculptor, which had stood on a high pedestal in the Hippodrome, and which Napoleon was to place for a time on the Arc de Triomphe. Two other wars were to see them displaced for safety and stabled with their great successors, the Gattamelata of Donatello and the Colleoni of Verrocchio, those equestrian monuments for which the Byzantine steeds had been a direct and powerful inspiration.

RELICS

For the crusaders loot took another form. To our lettered age, the insatiable desire for relics is one of the most remote phenomena of the Middle Ages, even if still today amongst the less sophisticated there is a cult of souvenirs, a dim descendant of the reigning medieval passion. But relics were no mere memorials. To men whose imaginations were untouched by the rich interchange of reading, these bones and fragments brought a new awareness of the life of Christ and the doings of the saints. They were tangible facts, and a splinter of the True Cross was more vivid in its mental stimulus than the Gospel accounts of the Passion or even the carved and painted crucifixes in the village church. The possession of a relic was something that penetrated into the intense localism of the time, bringing a direct experience which nothing else could supply. There were, needless to say, other and lower motives for their acquisition. A great cleric, while aware of their powers of edification, must also have known that they brought donations to his abbey or cathedral. Civic pride boasted of the divine protectors whose remains were locally possessed and competed to outdo its neighbours in these pious exhibits. The artist who noted the strange Eastern stuff in which the bones were wrapped or the reliquaries in which they were encased was a being of a rarer, less inbred sensibility.

To list the relics which can be definitely associated with the crusades would be a lengthy business. References to them are frequent in the chronicles, and they constantly appear as items in later inventories of church treasures. The sack of Constantinople brought the richest booty of all, and the famous account of the methodical search carried out by Martin, abbot of the monastery of Pairis in Alsace,[5] who did not scruple to *extend his sacred hands to rapine,* or *to commit sacrilege for sacred things,* is one of the most vivid pages in the story of this strange craving. At a later date, relics surviving from the siege became the main resource of the Latin emperors in their appeal for assistance, and the Sainte Chapelle of St. Louis received from Baldwin II the Sacred Lance, the Sponge, and the Crown of Thorns. The baton of the chapel's verger was a Byzantine wand of office, surmounted by a bust in sardonyx, based on the great statue of Constantine, which stood in the forum of his city and which in itself was a giant reliquary, for in the rays around its head were set the nails of the Crucifixion. In Rome the church of Sta. Prassede has a fragment of the column of the Flagellation, brought from Jerusalem by Cardinal Colonna in 1223; the iron ring from it was sent to St. Louis. This column caused some bewilderment for there was another column of the Flagellation in the Church of the Holy Sepulchre and yet another at Constantinople. In the iconography of the Counter-Reformation it is the short column of Sta. Prassede which is represented and which becomes the basis of a new rendering of Christ's scourging. Another Roman column, the famous spiral pillar treasured at St. Peter's as coming from the Temple, is Roman fourth-century work. Its prestige however made it a visual symbol of some importance, constantly echoed in Cosmati work. Raphael used it as the basis of his Beautiful Gate in one of the tapestry cartoons, and from there it became a popular element in the Baroque style. Even more remarkable a transit from the East was that of the sacred house of Loreto, said to have been borne by angels from Nazareth at the time of the final loss of the Holy Land. The little hut, encased in High Renaissance carving, can hardly claim an archaeologically convincing status, but there is a happy daring in its selection as the patronal shrine of the Italian Air Force. Meanwhile the ordinary pilgrim contented himself with much lesser things. William Wey, the fellow of Eton who twice, in 1458 and 1462, *passed over the See on peregrinage to Jerusalem,* left in his will a reliquary of boxwood containing six stones, one from Mt. Calvary, one from the Sepulchre, one from Mt. Tabor, one from the pillar to which Our Lord was fastened, one from the place where the Cross was hid, and one from the Holy Cave of Bethlehem.[6]

Greatest relic of all was the city of Jerusalem, *the haven of salvation, the place where His feet have stood.* It could not be stolen away, though its stonework was chipped off and even the earth piously dug up, but it could be described, its chief shrines could be copied and it could be mapped and drawn. It would be hard to overestimate the influence and popularity of these pilgrims' accounts. Dating from long before the crusades, they became in the twelfth century more exact and more critical. Access was then easy and no sites barred. In the earlier accounts the exhaustive credulity is at times surprising. The Bordeaux Pilgrim, visiting the city in 333, described *the stone that the builders rejected* (the great corner stone of the south-east angle of the Ḥarām wall, still today an impressive block) and the sycamore tree climbed by Zacchaeus.[7] Such over-precise enumeration continues into the crusading period, but there is a new interest in investigation. Serious thought was devoted to the competing claims of different sites, such as the dispute over the course of the Via Dolorosa. John of Würzburg, who was in Jerusalem about 1170, shews a real interest in establishing the facts: he notes for instance that Saffūriyah is claimed for the birthplace of the Virgin, but that Jerome states she was born at Nazareth; that the Baptist was buried at Sebastia, but executed at Machaerunta; that his body was burned by Julian the Apostate, but that the head was preserved, taken to Alexandria and later to Constantinople, whereas the forefinger with which he pointed out 'the Lamb of God' was taken by St. Thecla into the Alps and so came to be preserved at the church of St. Jean de Maurienne; that there are many difficulties in considering Mary of Bethany as the same person as Mary Magdalene; that Adam could not have been buried beneath Calvary because he was buried at Hebron. The last passage with its essay in iconographical interpretation is worth quoting. *As our Lord was thus dying on the cross, and of His own will giving up the ghost, the veil of the Temple was rent from the top to the bottom, and the rock in which the cross was fixed was split through the midst, in the place where it was touched by His blood; through which rent the blood flowed to the lower parts, wherein Adam is said to have been buried, and who was thus baptized in the blood of Christ. It is said to be in commemoration of this that a skull is always represented in paintings at the foot of the Cross; but this baptism of Adam in the blood of Christ means nothing more than that Adam was redeemed by the blood of Christ, since the Scripture tells us that he was buried at Hebron. It is rather Death and destruction which is personified by the hideous human face which is wont to be painted beneath the feet of the crucified One, because our Lord said, 'O Death, I will be thy death', that is, thy destruction.*[8]

MODELS OF
THE HOLY
SEPULCHRE

The stimulus given by pilgrims' accounts of the Holy Places led to the construction of models of them in the West. Chief shrine of all was the tomb of Christ in the Rotunda of the Church of the Holy Sepulchre. The oldest copy of this, though frequently restored, is probably that in the church of San Stefano at Bologna. By tradition this group of buildings, which formed a New Jerusalem including the main sites of the Passion, was founded by S. Petronio in the fifth century. Destroyed by the Huns in 903 it was rebuilt by Abbot Landulf in 1180. A contemporary chronicle states that the abbot devoted *special care to the reproduction of the Lord's Sepulchre, setting out the work himself with a measuring reed, for he had passed many days in Judaea collecting all the vestiges of Christian antiquity.*[9] The church itself is a dodecagon; the tomb chamber has an altar on the top approached by two staircases. It has been largely restored but may represent an early pre-crusading work. In France the church of Neuvy-Saint-Sépulchre was founded in 1045 (though the existing work is probably twelfth-century) *ad formam Sancti Sepulcri Ierosolimitani;* it is a rotunda with side tribunes; the central shrine has gone. By 1079 it was paying tithe to the Church of the Sepulchre in Jerusalem. The round church of St. Bénigne at Dijon, built by William of Volpiano in 1001, may have been another imitation, as also the rotunda at Charroux in Poitou, consecrated in 1095, of which only the central piers and the lantern, standing unbuttressed and magnificent, still remain. In Spain at Segovia the church of La Vera Cruz is a dodecagon building with a single aisle; within the central row of pillars is a model of the sepulchre, a two-storied building with steps going up to it as at Bologna. This was a Templars' chapel, built in 1208, and certainly is intended as a model of the Jerusalem church. It is interesting as an example of a polygonal not circular copy, which from the tomb chamber in its midst must represent the Rotunda, not the Templars' own church, the octagonal *Templum Domini* or Dome of the Rock. In France the

Templar chapel at Laon is octagonal; the Paris Temple church was circular. In England there were several examples of such churches, at Cambridge, Dover, Garway, Northampton, Little Maplestead, West Thurrock, Thetford, Temple Bruer, the priory church of St. John, Clerkenwell, and the Old and New Temple churches in London. These were, in some cases still are, round churches and the circle rather than the polygon seems to have been the favoured English shape. In no English instance does a copy of the tomb chamber still exist. In South Italy at Brindisi the Romanesque church of S. Giovanni al Sepolcro, also known as dei Templari and dei Cavalieri Gerosolimitani, is a circular church with a projecting apse. If 1045 can be taken as the foundation date for Neuvy-Saint-Sépulchre, it appears that a custom, which preceded the crusades, gained momentum with their preaching and expeditions. Under the patronage of the military orders several such chapels were built in the twelfth century, the period in which they were most numerous. Later examples are on a simpler scale. The chapel *made to the lykness of the sepulkyr of owre Lorde at Jerusalem* which William Wey set up at the Priory Church of Edington in Wiltshire has disappeared and it is unlikely that it was a main architectural feature of the church. Certainly the Chapel of Calvary, the Church of Bethlehem, and the Mount of Olives, to which his will refers, were models in wood.

This grouping of small versions of the sites recalls the hill shrines of Italy where at Varallo, Varese and elsewhere, tableaux of the Passion are set in huts round which the faithful can go in mimic pilgrimage. The Sacro Monte of Varallo, dignified by the art of Gaudenzio Ferrari, was founded about 1480 by Bernardino Caimi, an Observantine Franciscan who had been in the Holy Land and who chose its position from its likeness to that of Jerusalem, though Samuel Butler wrote that the resemblance *is hardly greater than the famous one between Monmouth and Macedon.* **TABLEAUX OF THE PASSION**

In Florence the ceremony of the dove and the Holy Fire, modelled on that of Jerusalem, is still carried out at Easter, having traditionally been founded after the first crusade by Pazzino de' Pazzi, who brought back some stones from the Holy Sepulchre, still preserved in the church of SS. Apostoli. Another Florentine, Giovanni Rucellai, some time between 1461 and 1467, sent an expedition to the Holy Land in order to bring back the exact design and measurements of the Holy Sepulchre, so as to build a copy of it in the Rucellai chapel in the church of San Pancrazio. This work is still there and Vasari tells us that the architect was Leon Battisti Alberti: with its Renaissance pilasters, ornamental parapet and roundels and boldly lettered inscription of the angel's words to the women, it is doubtful that, except in scale where it seems an accurate reduction, it bears any close resemblance to the Sepulchre, even though there is no complete certainty as to the exact form of the latter before its restoration in 1555 and the drawings of it published by Bernardo Amico. Amico provides his plan explicitly that anyone who wishes may *make use of the scale and make it of whatever material he pleases without too much labour.* The last phase of this Florentine devotion was the attempt of Ferdinand I in 1603 with the assistance of the Druse emir, Fakhr-ad-Dīn, to steal the Sepulchre itself, bring it to Florence and set it up in the Medici chapel at S. Lorenzo. A Florentine mission actually began to take down the tomb and was only foiled after a brawl in the church. **FLORENCE**

The concept of the chief sites and churches was by now firmly fixed in the Western mind. The frontispiece of a sixteenth-century copy of a *Histoire de Godefroi de Bouillon* (Brit. Mus. MS. Royal 17 F. v) shows the Temple as a round-domed building with supporting circular chapels. In Mantegna's Agony in the Garden, the large round church just within the walls, with the hill falling away beneath and then rising from the valley to Gethsemane, is topographically accurate, though the building has little exact resemblance to the Dome of the Rock; to Perugino or Raphael the Temple was, more correctly, a domed octagonal building standing in a paved court. Fifteenth-century Flemish painters, **THE TEMPLE IN ART** with their eagerness for realism, produced some striking buildings in their attempt to give visual effect to reports of the Dome of the Rock.

GORDON'S TOMB      The end of the nineteenth century saw an even more curious episode, the invention of a new tomb. A rock-cut tomb was found in 1867 on the hillside outside the Damascus gate. From symbols on it, it had obviously been used by Christians, but it is probably of a pre-Christian date. The garden in front of the tomb was cleared, and the site gained the name of Gordon's Tomb, through the fact that the General used it much for meditation when in Palestine in 1880. In the rocky face close by, two caves give something of the impression of a skull, and claims were made that this hillside was Golgotha, nicknamed the place of the skull from this rock formation. In 1892 a body of Anglican contributors purchased the site of the tomb and founded an association to maintain it: well cared for, with a pleasant, well planted garden, it is a peaceful spot, and could not be more unlike the crowded, ill-kept and tawdrily embellished Church of the Holy Sepulchre. Anglican good taste has here its Jerusalem stronghold, and if its claims to authenticity are slight, its restfulness has been welcome to many. It is a  place of quiet after the high passions which Jerusalem can so powerfully intensify.

# BIBLIOGRAPHY

Much has been written on the Holy Land, and it is only possible here to give a brief list of the more recent and basic works. Relevant extracts from chronicles and pilgrims' accounts can be found in D. Baldi, *Enchiridion Locorum Sanctorum* (Jerusalem, 1935).

## General
M. van Berchem and E. Fatio, *Voyage en Syrie* (3 vols., Cairo 1915); L.-H. Vincent and F.-M. Abel, *Jerusalem* II (Paris 1914–26); C. N. Johns, *Palestine of the Crusades: Map and Gazetteer* (Survey of Palestine, 1946); A. Ben-Horin and M. Avi-Jonah, *Map of Palestine during the period of the Crusades* (Introduction and notes in Hebrew: Jerusalem 1960); *The Legacy of Islam*, ed. G. T. Arnold and A. Guillaume (1931).

## Churches
M. de Vogüé, *Églises de la Terre Sainte* (Paris 1860); C. Enlart, *Les Monuments des Croisés dans le Royaume de Jérusalem: Architecture religieuse et civile* (2 vols., 2 albums of plates, Paris 1928).

## Castles
G. Rey, *Étude sur les Monuments de l'Architecture militaire des Croisés en Syrie et dans l'Ile de Chypre* (Paris 1871); P. Deschamps, *Les Châteaux des Croisés en Terre Sainte:* I *Le Crac des Chevaliers* (text and album, Paris 1934); II *La défense du Royaume de Jérusalem* (text and album, Paris 1939); R. C. Smail, *Crusading Warfare 1097–1193* (Cambridge 1956); R. Fedden and J. Thomson, *Crusader Castles* (London 1957); W. Müller-Wiener, *Castles of the Crusaders* (London 1966).

Some more specialised works are given in the notes. The general history of the Crusades is admirably treated by Sir Steven Runciman in his 3 vols., *A History of the Crusades.* (London 1951–54)

## Abbreviations
RHC = Recueil des Historiens des Croisades Occ. (Occidentaux) et Or. (Orientaux)
DAP = Department of Antiquities, Palestine
PPTS = Palestine Pilgrim Text Society

# NOTES

## I. Jerusalem

1 Burchard of Mount Sion, *Description of the Holy Land* (PPTS, 1896), p. 1.

2 Arculf, *The Churches of the Holy Land* (PPTS, 1891), pp. 29–34.

3 George Sandys, *Travels* (7th edit., 1673), p. 125.

4 Eusebius, *Life of Constantine* (Greek ecclesiastical historians I, 1845), p. 136. See A. W. Clapham, 'The Latin Monastic Buildings of the Church of the Holy Sepulchre', *Antiquaries Journal* I (1921) pp. 3–18.

5 *Recueil des Historiens de la France* X, p. 51.

6 *Revue de l'Orient latin* III (1895), p. 186.

7 *The Itineraries of William Wey* (Roxburghe Club, 1857), p. xxix.

8 Munich, Staatsbibliothek MS. 2967.

9 Sandys, *Travels*, p. 125.

10 Ludolph of Suchem, *Description of the Holy Land* (PPTS, 1895), p. 103.

11 A. de Lamartine, *Souvenirs, Impressions, Pensées et Paysages, pendant un voyage en Orient, 1832–1833* (1835), p. 150.

12 J. Strzygowski, 'Ruins of Tombs of the Latin Kings', *Speculum* XI (1936), pp. 499–508.

13 John of Würzburg, *Description of the Holy Land* (PPTS, 1890), p. 27.

14 C. N. Johns, *Guide to the Citadel of Jerusalem* (DAP, 1944); and *Quarterly of DAP*, V (1935), pp. 127–131 and X (1950), pp. 121–190.

## II. The Travellers

1 H. W. Davies, *Bernhard von Breydenbach and his journey to the Holy Land* (1911).

2 Sandys, *Travels*, p. 124.

3 William Lithgow, *A most delectable and true Discourse, of an admired and paineful Peregrination from Scotland to the most famous Kingdoms in Europe, Asia and Affricke* (1614) (no pagination).

4 Corneille le Bruyn, *A Voyage to the Levant*, done into English by W. J. (1702), p. 1.

5 H. Maundrell, *A Journey from Aleppo to Jerusalem at Easter, A.D. 1697* (1703), Preface.

6 Richard Pococke, *A Description of the East*, 2 vols. (1743–5), II. pp. 63, 200, 201.

7 E. D. Clarke, *Travels in various Countries of Europe, Asia and Africa*, II (1812), pp. 407, 462, 533, 560.

8 F.-R. de Chateaubriand, *Itinéraire de Paris à Jérusalem*, 2 vols. (1812) II, p. 20.

9 T. R. Jolliffe, *Letters from Palestine* (1819), p. 41.

10 *Report of Four Lectures delivered at Banbury Mechanics Institute*, Jan. 1837 (1837).

11 J. S. Buckingham, *Travels in Palestine* (1821), pp. XV, XIX.

12 A. Barry, *Memoir of Sir Charles Barry* (1867).

13 L. de Laborde, *Voyage de la Syrie* (1837), p. 3.

14 W. Bartlett, *Walks about the City and Environs of Jerusalem* (1855), p. 162.

15 M. de Vogüé, *Le Temple de Jérusalem* (1864), p. 47.

16 A. Cunningham, *Life of Sir David Wilkie* (1843) III, p. 416.

17 J.-F. Michaud, *Histoire des Croisades* (1862) I, p. IV.

## III. The Castles

1 J. C. M. Laurent, *Peregrinatores Medii Aevi Quattuor* (1864), pp. 169, 170.

2 L. de Laborde, *Voyage de la Syrie* (1837), p. 25.

3 W. K. Kelly, *Syria and the Holy Land* (1844), p. 129.

4 F. de Saulcy, *Narrative of a Journey round the Dead Sea and in the Bible Lands* (1854) II, p. 499.

5 R. Pococke, *A Description of the East* II (1745), p. 57.

6 Kelly, *op. cit.*, p. 103.

7 *Historia Francorum qui ceperunt Jerusalem*, RHC Occ. II, p. 239.

8 H. Hagenmeyer, *Die Kreuzzugsbriefe* (1961), p. 139.

9 *Historia rerum in partibus transmarinis gestarum* (trs. E. A. Babcock: Records of Civilization, XXXV, 2 vols. 1943), II pp. 130, 131, 373.

10 *Livre des deux Jardins*, RCH Or. IV, pp. 387, 388; see F.-M. Abel, *Revue Biblique* 1912, pp. 405–409.

11 *History* II, pp. 58, 130, 131.

12 *Crusader Castles* (1936) II, p. 60. For Saone see articles by Paul Deschamps in *Gazette des Beaux-Arts* IV (1930), pp. 329–364, and *Syria* XVI (1935), pp. 73–88.

13 Baha' ad-Din, *The Life of Saladin* (PPTS, 1879), p. 130.

14 *The Travels of Ibn Jubayr*, trs. R. J. C. Broadhurst (1952), p. 268.

15 D. J. C. King, 'The Taking of Le Krak des Chevaliers', *Antiquity* XXIII (1949), pp. 83–92.

16 Quoted in C. N. Johns, *Guide to ʿAtlit* (DAP, 1947), p. 17.

17 Hon. Charles Irby and James Mangles, *Travels in Egypt, and Nubia, Syria, and Asia Minor 1817 and 1818*, p. 191.

18 *The History of St. Louis*, trs. Joan Evans (1937), pp. 107 and 116; (trs. J. Hutton, 1910) p. 164.

19 *Bulletin of the Metropolitan Museum of Art* (1927), Part II.

[20] Burchard of Mount Sion, *Description of the Holy Land*, PPTS (1896), p. 11.

[21] Louis Lortet, *La Syrie d'aujourd'hui 1875–1880* (1884), p. 52.

[22] Laurent, *Peregrinatores*, p. 167.

[23] John Madox, *Excursions in the Holy Land* (1834) II, p. 79.

[24] Quoted in Deschamps, *Krac*, p. 100.

[25] V. Guérin, *Description de la Palestine: Galilée* (1880) II, pp. 419–426.

[26] Marquis de Vogüé, *Syrie, Palestine, Mt. Athos* (1876), p. 101.

[27] William of Tyre, *History* I, p. 506.

[28] C. N. Johns, 'Mediaeval Ajlun', *Quarterly DAP*, I (1931), pp. 21–33.

[29] P. K. Hitti, *Memoirs of an Arab-Syrian Gentleman* (1927), p. 98.

[30] *History of St. Louis* (trs. Evans), pp. 94–96; (trs. J. Hutton, 1910), pp. 128–132.

[31] A. de Lamartine, *Souvenirs*, p. 80.

[32] J. W. Hackett, 'Saladin's Campaign of 1188 in Northern Syria' (unpublished thesis, Oxford 1937).

[33] See articles by M. Gough, J. G. Dunbar and W. W. M. Boal, and G. R. Youngs in *Anatolian Studies* II (1952), pp. 119–125; XIV (1964), pp. 175–194; XV (1965), pp. 113–134.

### IV. The Churches

[1] See R. W. Hamilton, 'The Church of the Nativity at Bethlehem', DAP (1947); B. Bagatti, *Gli antichi edifici sacri de Betlemme* (Jerusalem 1952).

[2] William of Tyre, *History*, I, p. 55.

[3] See L.-H. Vincent, E. J. H. Mackay and F.-M. Abel, *Hebron*, 2 vols. (1923) pp. 166–183.

[4] Irby and Mangles, *Travels*, p. 361.

[5] R. W. Hamilton, *Guide to Samaria-Sebaste* (DAP, 1944).

[6] See P. Viaud, *Nazareth* (1910), and B. Bagatti, 'Ritrovamenti nella Nazaret evangelica', *Studi Biblici Franciscani Liber Annuus V* (1954–55).

[7] Jean Doubdan, *Le Voyage de la Terre-Sainte* (1661), p. 485.

[8] P. Deschamps, *Monuments et Mémoires Piot* XXXI (1930), pp. 99–118, and XXXII (1932), pp. 119–126.

[9] *Athenaeum Journal* (1847), p. 339 and information in the manuscript catalogue at Chatsworth.

[10] Maundrell, *A Journey from Aleppo to Jerusalem*, p. 19.

[11] Joinville, *History* (trs. Evans), p. 124.

[12] Ludolph of Suchem, *Description of the Holy Land* (PPTS, 1895), p. 50. N. Makhouly and C. N. Johns, *Guide to Acre* (DAP, 1946).

[13] All discussion of crusading illumination is dependent on H. Buchthal, *Miniature Painting in the Latin Kingdom of Jerusalem* (Oxford 1957), which revealed a whole new field of study.

[14] K. Weitzmann, 'Thirteenth century crusading icons on Mount Sinai', *The Art Bulletin* XLV (1963), pp. 179–203.

[15] M. van Berchem and E. Fatio, *Voyage en Syrie* (1913), I, p. 240.

[16] Maundrell, *Journey from Aleppo*, p. 28.

### V. East and West

[1] C. Enlart, 'L'église du Wast en Boulonnais', *Gazette des Beaux-Arts* (1927), pp. 1–11.

[2] V. Mortet, *Recueil de textes relatifs à l'histoire d'architecture* I (1911), pp. 183, 332, 355.

[3] *The Conquest of Constantinople*, ed. E. H. McNeal (Records of Civilization XXIII, 1936), pp. 102–113.

[4] *Narratio de Statuis Antiquis*, ed. F. Wilken (1830).

[5] P. Riant, *Exuviae sacrae constantinopolitanae* (1881) I, pp. 57–126.

[6] *The Itineraries of William Wey* (Roxburghe Club, 1857), p. xxix.

[7] Bordeaux Pilgrim, *An Itinerary* (trs. Aubrey Stewart) (PPTS, 1896), pp. 20, 25.

[8] *Description of the Holy Land*, PPTS, p. 32.

[9] Quoted in G. Jeffery, *The Holy Sepulchre* (1919), p. 197.

In the extracts quoted from translations I have in some instances altered the wording.

# LIST OF ILLUSTRATIONS

(Those marked * are coloured)

# INDEX OF PLACES

Page numbers shown thus *(34)* refer to illustrations

a